THE WORD I HAVE NEVER LEARNED

A Tale of Two Souls

VENKATESH VEERANKI

For permission requests, write to the publisher at: venkya2z@gmail.com

Table of Contents

Some children grow up without love. Some grow up afraid to name it...

Preface

In the tapestry of life, a mother's warmth is meant to nurture, while a father's steady presence is meant to protect. These two forces—care and security—form the invisible foundation upon which a child's happiness, confidence, and sense of belonging are built. When even one parent embraces this responsibility with love and wisdom, a child is given the chance to grow, to dream, and to thrive in a world that is anything but predictable.

And yet, some may ask: what of children who grow up without parents? Many orphans find strength in solitude and rise through the sheer force of will. But what is often overlooked is that the damage caused by toxic parents and a fractured family can run deeper than the absence of family itself. Neglect, emotional abandonment, and manipulation can cast shadows that follow a child long after childhood is over—shadows darker and more enduring than silence.

A family's love is often seen as the most unconditional and pure form of affection. When a child grows up feeling unloved by their own family, it can shatter their sense of security and belonging. This absence leaves deep emotional scars, making it difficult for them to trust others and often leading them to spend their entire lives searching for the true meaning of love, friendship, home, and happiness.

This is the story of a boy navigating that darkness. A boy burdened not only by fear, anxiety, and self-doubt, but also by the weight of being constantly overlooked, misunderstood, and used. His life is shaped by absence, not in the literal sense, but in the haunting presence of those who failed to show up in the ways that mattered.

From an early age, he witnessed more loss than most do in a lifetime. Death, both literal and emotional, became a silent companion—whispering that his pain might never be seen, his voice never heard. But this is not a tale of surrender. It is a quiet rebellion, a slow and painful awakening to the truth that living well is not about chasing immortality or fearing death every day. It is about preparing, with courage and clarity, to meet the inevitable with dignity—and to build a life that feels like his own, one honest breath at a time.

Through loneliness and resilience, through grief and moments of hard-won hope, this is a journey toward understanding what it truly means to have a family, to feel at home, and to finally learn what love might look like—not in fantasy, but in fragments of reality….

Unveiling Shadows: Broken by Birth

Today, after a long period of silence, I confided in a co-worker who, having just received his transfer order, will soon be leaving. I always knew that sharing one's problems, even if the listener can't offer a solution, can make us feel better. But I never realized it could feel this good, and there's a reason for that, which I hope you'll discover in the coming chapters. My co-worker couldn't offer a miraculous solution—no one can—but he made an earnest effort to understand my situation.

After my shift, I hurried back to my quarters on my scooty. As I slowly opened my bedroom door, Dolly calmly emerged from behind it. I was just hoping she hadn't vomited this time. When she saw me, she let out a long "Meowwww." I felt relieved seeing no hairballs or vomit. I gave her some water and fed her chicken paste before having some bread toast for breakfast myself.

Taking care of a small kitten like Dolly, whom I chose to bring home, makes me realize the immense responsibility involved. It makes me think about how much more responsible one must be when bringing a child into this world. I often compare myself to her in these moments, and a thousand thoughts and questions flood my mind each time.

Simply articulating my primary concerns to someone brought me immense relief. With the thought that even one person truly understanding me would bring profound happiness, I decided to pen down my story.

Most people's stories begin with their birth, family background, or childhood. However, my story began even before my birth and would be incomplete without knowing about my ancestors, starting with my grandparents.

In a small town in Andhra Pradesh, Raghavayya, a stationmaster, lived with his wife, Savitri, and their eight children. Yes, eight children. They even had a ninth child who, sadly, died as an infant (or maybe he was lucky). It was the era of baby boomers, and having a large family was quite common back then.

The problem with Raghavayya and Savitri wasn't just the number of children, but how they planned to raise them. Among the five sisters and three brothers, the eldest daughter, Chandrika, the third eldest daughter, Kalyani, and the eldest son, Ramachandra, managed to complete their studies and secured government jobs. Ramachandra and Kalyani got married and started their own families, while the other siblings remained dependent on their father or Chandrika, who stayed unmarried to support her family.

The second daughter, Nirmala, married a Central Government employee and had two daughters. The fourth daughter, Sarala, married a High Court employee, also a heavy drinker, and they had three daughters. Geetha, the fifth sister, is currently living with her parents and is unemployed. Despite her parents arranging many matches for her, she remains unmarried (at this time). The youngest son, Srinivas, became mentally challenged at a very young age and continued to live with his parents.

Now, who remained unaccounted for? It was the second brother, Kiran. In a family of this size, it was often difficult to keep track of everyone. Kiran had neither completed his education nor pursued any productive employment. He continued to live with their parents, managing a modest photocopy shop that had been set up with financial support from Chandrika.

When raising multiple children, it is essential to foster values like brotherhood and the deeper meaning of family. Raghavayya completely failed in this regard, and to cover up the repercussions of his actions, he made even more mistakes. Chandrika chose to remain unmarried, which could have been her personal choice, but everyone has dreams and aspirations for their own life. Raghavayya, knowingly or unknowingly, burdened Chandrika with the responsibility of his other children: one being mentally ill, one being too lazy to earn a living, and the others who viewed her as a cash cow with no one to spend her hard-earned money on except her siblings.

On the other hand, Kiran, who had never understood the value of hard work and money, decided to get married, thinking that an educated wife could support the family with her earnings. How unfortunate! Savitri's brother offered his daughter, Deepa, to marry Kiran, despite being aware of his situation. But who would offer their daughter to a man with no qualifications or income?

Raghavayya, despite his education, failed to grasp the consequences of his actions on his family. Perhaps, in his youthful immaturity, he had all these children without considering the future. Now, faced with reality, he is trying to patch things up and evade his responsibilities. Consequently, he decided to marry Kiran to Deepa.

Savitri's brother, Ramesh Rao, who is Deepa's father, lived in Visakhapatnam. Deepa had an elder sister and a younger brother. Kiran's elder sister, Nirmala, also resided in Visakhapatnam and was married to Suresh. Upon learning that Kiran's marriage was arranged with Deepa, Suresh wrote a letter to Raghavayya, advising against the marriage. He cited reasons such as Deepa and her mother's unpredictable behavior and the chaotic situation in their household.

However, despite these concerns, Raghavayya was swayed by the B. Ed certificate of Deepa presented by Ramesh Rao and a small dowry. Coupled with his indecisiveness, he chose not to call off the marriage, and Kiran ended up marrying Deepa.

Meanwhile, Sarala's husband, Vijayendra, concocted a story about being betrayed by his friends and suffering financial losses. He sent their two elder daughters (out of three) to live with Raghavayya and Savitri, with support from Chandrika.

Deepa's unpredictable nature gradually became apparent. She stole money and food from the household and frequently got into cat-fights with her mother-in-law, Savitri. Additionally, she neglected her personal hygiene, refused to help with cooking or other household chores, and often exhibited laziness and aggressive tantrums.

Kiran eventually discovered that Deepa's B. Ed certificate was fraudulent, realizing it was a cunning ploy by Ramesh Rao to marry off his troublesome daughter. Despite this, Kiran remained passive, failing to take the necessary action. His lack of foresight and the misguided fear of societal judgment, worrying that people would mock him, made him remain silent.

Ramachandra, despite being the eldest son and working in the government sector, remained under the control of his wife (who was Suresh's sister) after marriage and had two children, a girl and a boy. He lived separately from his parents and siblings.

Chandrika now supported her ailing parents, an unmarried sister, a mentally challenged brother, a lazy brother with his troublesome wife, and the children of another sister. All of them relied on her financially. Chandrika's decision to remain single did not trouble her parents and siblings. Perhaps they were comforted knowing her earnings wouldn't go to a husband. Instead, she generously supported her family and treated her siblings' children as her own. Unconcerned with traditional family structures, she discovered happiness within herself. Little did she know how this would affect her life later on.

Chandrika's biggest worry was about Kiran and Deepa. Deepa was a woman who preferred laziness, neglected her hygiene, and even stole from the household. Kiran, meanwhile, was a man who lacked a sense of life's purpose, had no understanding of the value of money, and showed little regard for hard work. Savitri and others ridiculed him for failing to manage his wife, while some considered Deepa fortunate to have a passive, society-fearing husband. That might make Kiran a tolerant husband—but did it make him a good father? Definitely not.

As the days turned into weeks, Chandrika remained engrossed in her work, tirelessly earning to support her parents and siblings. She was oblivious to the gradual unraveling of her family's circumstances. During this time, Deepa gave birth to a baby boy. That boy is me.

Whispers of fate and misfortune echoed through the family, carried by the words of a distant elderly relative who knew the intricate histories of Kiran, Deepa, and Raghavayya's family. With a voice heavy with foreboding, he declared, "This boy is cursed to be born."

Divine Intervention or Devil's Hand?

Like a fragile doll in the hands of immature children playing a game dictated by society, I faced my first trial within days of my birth. In the city of Visakhapatnam, Deepa, still in her paternal home, fed me an oil meant for her father's aching feet. The mistake nearly cost me my life. Yet, against all odds, I clung to life. Meanwhile, Kiran, despite knowing that Deepa had given birth to a son, remained in his hometown. Savitri's indifference kept him from visiting his wife and newborn. It was only after hearing about Deepa's near-fatal mistake that he decided to act. He traveled to bring both Deepa and me back home, more out of a sense of duty than responsibility.

As an infant, I was kept in an environment surrounded by people like Savitri, who despised my mother, and Raghavayya, who spent his days chain-smoking and listening to music in his room. Kiran spent his days idly at a photocopy shop, earning just enough for Deepa to steal at night. Srinivas, who suffered from mental illness, wandered the streets and sometimes picked random spots to answer nature's call. Additionally, my cousins, Shambavi and Eswari (daughters of Sarala), and Geetha, Savitri's youngest daughter, also stayed in the same house.

I often found myself on the sidelines, watching my cousins as they began to talk and interact with the world around them. Unlike them, I had no one to guide me through my early steps or encourage my first words. While my cousins received plenty of attention and support, my development was left to chance. As a result, by the time I turned two, I still hadn't spoken a word.

Then, one day, Sarala's husband, Vijayendra, brought an Ayurvedic medicine called Saraswati Churna for his daughters to enhance their cognitive abilities. However, it seems I ended up consuming most of it, leaving very little for my cousins. Shortly after, I began to speak.

As mentioned earlier, a mother nurtures and a father protects—nurturing includes providing proper care and habits, while protection ensures physical and emotional safety. Across the animal kingdom, including humans, observing and imitating parents is vital for learning key survival skills like feeding, socializing, and self-defense.

But when parents lack survival skills or good habits themselves, what can they offer their child to learn from? My mother ate junk food like chocolates, biscuits, and soft drinks, using money she stole from the household, and fed me the same from a very young age. She didn't teach me any good habits. I was bullied by my so-called blood relatives because of my mother, and my father never cared about how this affected my growth. The word "mother" taunts me the most, to the point that since I became aware of my surroundings, I have never called my mother "amma." I don't know whether to blame my mother, the people around me, or God for this.

Chandrika, who used to work in a nearby town, would occasionally visit our house, sending money and providing financial support to her parents and siblings whenever needed. Despite being taken to many hospitals, Srinivas's mental condition remained unchanged. Amidst all this, Raghavayya mostly stayed calm, enjoying his post-retirement life in his room, listening to music and smoking. At this point, He has Chandrika, who earns, Geetha, who is still unmarried and helps with household chores, and Kiran, who takes care of tasks that traditionally require a man, such as getting groceries and assisting with electrical and plumbing work. Occasional cat-fights between Savitri and Geetha on one side and Deepa on the other had become a daily routine, and everyone had somewhat gotten used to this way of living.

After my birth, Deepa found herself pregnant several times. However, Chandrika firmly advised my father against having more children, pointing to their precarious financial situation as the reason.

In addition to these complexities, my family has a peculiar habit of frequently using medications without consulting a doctor. They tend to overlook natural healing methods and rely on medicines for even minor issues. Natural healing methods require good lifestyle habits and patience, as they take time to show results. Consequently, due to a certain level of laziness, everyone in this family tends to resort to medications, which has unfortunately led to a pattern resembling drug abuse.

Srinivas, who had mental health issues, had been prescribed sleeping pills to help manage his tantrums. However, Deepa—who had a strong inclination toward medications—would often steal and take those pills herself. As a result, she would fall into a deep sleep and neglect her household responsibilities.

As an infant, I was left to grow under the care of fate, with my parents entrusting my upbringing to divine will. My grandmother viewed me not as a child, but as the offspring of a woman they despised. Meanwhile, the rest of my relatives saw me as a rival, competing for a share of my Aunt

Chandrika's earnings, which they were determined to claim entirely for themselves.

From one perspective, my survival as an infant in such an environment seems like a miraculous act of divine intervention. However, from another angle, it feels as though a malevolent evil force has thrust me into a challenging adulthood, where I must face the repercussions of my family's dysfunction—burdens for which I bear no responsibility.

Fragments of Childhood: My Earliest Recollections

Everything I've shared so far is pieced together from what I've learned from others who witnessed my early years of childhood amnesia. My first vivid memory is of my first day at school. Perhaps this is a common experience, or maybe it stands out because of the neglect and isolation I faced, being kept inside the house without any social interaction or care.

On my first day of school too, the only moment I remember is stepping into the classroom as my father left me there. I was screaming, not because I was being left behind, but out of sheer excitement for the new books. I was so captivated by the idea of holding new books and their fresh smell that I cried incessantly until I finally had a book in my hands.

Later in my kindergarten days, I fondly remember playing games where balloons were tied to our feet as we ran around. During lunch, my grandmother would bring food for my cousins and me—curd rice with pomegranate seeds, a dish that remains my favorite to this day. Back then, I saw her as a loving woman who prepared delicious meals for her grandchildren. However, as I reflect on those memories and connect them with later events in my life, I perceive her in a very different way.

Both of my cousins, who are a few years older than me, lived in the same house until I was in the third grade. After that, they moved to Hyderabad to live with their parents. My grandmother never visited my school at lunchtime with food after they left. Reflecting on this, I realize that the love I experienced might have been an illusion, intended more for my cousins, who were her daughter's children, rather than for me.

From a very young age, I witnessed constant quarrels between Deepa and Savitri in our household. My parents frequently moved back and forth between our house and a rented house, but I stayed with my grandparents. Reflecting on my childhood, I now realize how significantly my uncle Srinivas, who struggles with mental health, influenced my personality. He would wander around, talking to himself, and smoking rolled tobacco leaves, known as "Chutta," with my grandfather. Despite everything, he always greeted me with a gentle smile whenever he saw me. In fact, it was my uncle Srinivas—despite his mental illness—who once saved me when I fell off the asbestos roof of the storeroom attached to our house. I lost consciousness, my head was bleeding, and it was he who came to my rescue.

I believe my school days until I turned 10 were the only time in my life when, despite the troublesome and traumatic situations at home, I wasn't greatly affected. There are two reasons for this. First, ignorance—as they say, ignorance is bliss. I was too young to grasp the dysfunction in my family and the true intentions of those around me, and I had no reason to think about my future. Second, my grandfather, who, even being in his own world, tolerated all my childhood mischiefs without calling me names, unlike my grandmother or others.

Until my 2nd standard, I struggled academically, unable to grasp basic arithmetic, English, or Telugu grammar. However, no one at home was aware of this, perhaps because my parents never really paid attention to my physical and mental development. My aunt Chandrika only occasionally visited our house, as she was busy with her own work life in a different town. As a child, I viewed her as an angel who always brought new clothes and sweets whenever she visited. I recall asking her about her husband's whereabouts out of childish curiosity, to which she replied with a smile, "He lives in America."

I must admit, much of what I've learned in life came from doing the wrong things—simply because there was no one around to show me the right ones. From a young age, I had to figure things out on my own, often through trial and error.

I still remember the science fair in second grade. The teacher announced it with enthusiasm, explaining that each student would present something they had made. I didn't really understand what that meant. To me, it sounded like I needed to give her something—something she could show on my behalf. I told my father, and the next morning, instead of going straight to school, we skipped the first period and went to the market. We bought a small rubber elephant toy. I handed it to my teacher, and she accepted it with a kind smile in front of the others.

But on the day of the fair, I searched the room for my toy. It was nowhere to be seen. I finally gathered the courage to ask my teacher what had happened to it. She looked at me gently and said, "This is a science fair. Toys like that aren't meant to be displayed."

Her words were soft, but they cut deep. I felt embarrassed, confused—and for the first time, I became aware of the gap between me and the other children. As they proudly spoke about how their parents had helped them with their projects, I realized just how different my world was.

That day marked something quiet but lasting in me: the beginning of comparison. I never asked for the elephant back. Somehow, not asking felt easier than facing the shame all over again.

Later,in my 3rd grade, I attended tuition with my elder cousins, and miraculously, my academics and marks began to improve. By the 4th grade, for the first time, I developed an inclination towards studies and actually enjoyed reading books, especially those on general studies. I wasn't the top student, but I also wasn't someone who struggled with academics.

Once, during a leisure period, our PT sir, Mr. Gopal, asked us to draw something. I poured all my random imaginations onto the paper. To my surprise, he said, "You will become a great person." I really don't know what he saw in that, but this compliment is something I cherish to this day.

After my cousins moved to Hyderabad to live with their parents, I found joy in sneaking into my grandfather's room to explore his old archives without his permission, climbing trees in the backyard, and watching old movies on TV with my grandparents. These were the little adventures that filled my days at home as a lonely child without any guidance, unaware of what tomorrow may bring.

After several unsuccessful attempts at finding a match, Geetha, my youngest aunt and my father's youngest sister, finally married a businessman from a nearby town. This was the first wedding I ever witnessed, and throughout the ceremony, I stayed close to my aunt Chandrika. A few months later, while the whole family was eagerly watching the wedding video, news arrived of my maternal grandmother's passing. It was the first time I realized I had another grandmother living in Visakhapatnam. My father's side of the family disliked my mother so much that I was never told about her. My maternal grandfather had passed away long ago, when I was just an infant, I believe. Even then, I wasn't sent to Visakhapatnam to see her body, and to this day, I have no idea what my maternal grandmother looked like.

A major change in my academic performance occurred in the 5th grade. I was sent to another tuition with Kumari Miss (we called every teacher "Miss" back then). She was a brilliant math teacher, and her expertise and passion for the subject inspired me greatly. My grandfather would occasionally visit the tuition, and he would converse with her in English. Watching him speak made me feel both proud and inspired. I still vividly remember the moment when a math problem kept lingering in my mind. Suddenly, late at night, I found myself vigorously writing and thinking, determined to discover alternate solutions. A boy who once struggled with basic arithmetic has now become the class topper. But this happiness was short-lived; my life began to get complicated right after my 5th grade.

On the final day of my summer holidays after 5th grade, my grandfather called me into his room and told me not to go to school the next day. I happily agreed, thrilled that my summer break had been extended by my grandfather himself, and I rejoiced immensely. The next morning, when I woke up, my cousin, who was also there for the summer holidays, softly told me, "Grandfather has passed away."

The Silent Struggle: Prey to the Unfolding Reality

The man whose name our entire family is recognized by, who tolerated all my mischiefs and gave me pocket money for school, who made me feel special despite my dysfunctional parents, now lies motionless and dead. Many relatives, whose faces I had never seen before, gathered, and the one-day summer break extension my grandfather had given me stretched into almost 15-20 days.

Life suddenly felt very different. Kumari Miss was posted to a government job and left our school. When I returned to school, I tried to catch up on the missed topics in each subject, but it was quite challenging.

My second eldest aunt, Nirmala, recently lost her husband to liver cirrhosis caused by excessive alcohol consumption and her two daughters, who are a few years older than me, have moved from Visakhapatnam to our hometown, but they are living in a different rented house.

Then I became seriously ill and was admitted to the hospital. Initially, the doctors suspected appendicitis, so I was put on saline for several days while undergoing repeated scans and X-rays. At one point, a doctor mentioned I might have osteopoiesis. However, it turned out that I had neither appendicitis nor osteopoiesis. Although these medical terms didn't worry me much, it was frustrating to remain in the hospital even after I started feeling better, as the doctors still wouldn't discharge me.

The hospital bills were, of course, covered by my aunt Chandrika. My father never questioned why the doctors kept me as an inpatient. It's the doctors' business to treat patients and earn money, often taking advantage of their ignorance. If someone is truly concerned about money, they would question the necessity of treatments, seek a second opinion, or do their own research. However, my father didn't consider this perspective, as Aunt Chandrika was always there to support his negligent lifestyle financially.

Even after returning home from the hospital, I didn't go back to school right away. My mother began taking the sleeping pills meant for my mentally ill uncle, Srinivas, and spent most of her time in a state resembling that of a drug addict. My grandmother often targeted me verbally, mentioning my mother and Nirmala, who had moved to the same town, frequently visited and criticized me for being ill. Although I wasn't actually sick, I avoided face-to-face interactions with them by hiding under a blanket. This is when I began to develop social anxiety.

My aunt Chandrika worked in a different town, and with my grandfather no longer around, and my father just passing the time at his shop,I felt completely abandoned, with no one to care for my mental well-being. It was a lonely and overwhelming time, where I desperately needed support but found none.

I began to resent being with my mother, having been bullied in her name by everyone at home. People around me made me feel ashamed of being born to a woman they deemed unfit with physical and mental problems. This shame made me hesitant to call her "AMMA" in public, and over time, it turned into a fear of being judged whenever someone heard me call her that. I often wonder if any other child has ever faced such a situation.

I still recall someone, perhaps my grandmother or Sarala, sarcastically remarking that I drank my mother's milk until I was three years old, as if it were something to be ashamed of. It's not just being born to such a woman that was my problem, but also being raised in an environment where people were so cruel as to target a small child in such a malicious way.

Amid all this turmoil, my father seemed indifferent to how the situation at home was affecting his child. He spent his time running a photocopy shop, funded by my aunt Chandrika, without any thought for investing in his own future or mine. The little money he earned was either stolen by my mother or willingly handed over to her to appease her tantrums.

I don't want to blame my father for his actions or inactions, but if I were to summarize his qualities,he is someone who constantly compares his situation to others in society, yet fails to think critically or analyze what it truly takes to achieve success like others. Instead of taking proactive steps, he remains passive and unmotivated, lacking the drive to improve his circumstances.

He constantly finds someone else to blame for his own failures. For his unemployment, he blames my grandparents for sending him to a school with fewer resources, not realizing that success is more about willpower than education. At home, he blames his wife for their problems, but he doesn't acknowledge that marrying her was his choice, and if he truly wanted to, he could have chosen to divorce her.

When I returned to school, many of my classmates thought I had transferred to another school. With my developing social anxiety, it was difficult to cope, but I had no other choice. I didn't want to stay home and endure verbal criticism, so I pushed myself every day to face the reality at school, even though I felt alienated. It suddenly felt as if all my hidden fears—born from shyness, the harsh environment, cruel verbal abuse, and the lack of parental care and support—were unleashed upon me at once. Gradually, I developed a strange fear of facing people and reality. I didn't have the courage to approach Kumari Miss for tuition again, even though she repeatedly asked me to join through other students.

Navigating the Void Within: The Dawn of Self-Discovery

The experiences and observations you have in one place can significantly influence your behavior and reactions in another, especially during childhood. This impact can be profound in later life, particularly in the absence of parental care.

There was a government school right in front of my house where students from grades 6 to 10 studied in Telugu medium. Ever since my grandfather was alive, the schoolboys often played cricket on the school grounds. There were frequent conflicts between the schoolboys and my father and grandfather over balls being thrown into our house. Consequently, the schoolboys developed a habit of mocking us, particularly my uncle, who is mentally ill. I used to keep my distance from them.

Imagine a lonely child, mocked at home because of his mother and in the street because of his uncle, with no one to share his feelings with. This difficult home environment influenced my behavior at school.

I often felt isolated at school, wandering alone during intervals and avoiding sports. My classmates played cricket, but I had developed a deep-seated fear of being mocked by the school boys who played cricket in front of my house. Their taunts, especially towards my mentally ill uncle, left a lasting impact on me. As a result, I would sit idle or roam around alone during the sports period, feeling disconnected and anxious.

I went to school by rickshaw, and the rickshaw puller would bring my lunch from home every day. After my cousins moved to Hyderabad, my grandmother stopped coming to school with lunch. Instead, she would send a packed lunch box with the same lentils (pappu) and rice every day. Meanwhile, my classmates, who had different items each day, would sit together in groups, eating and sharing their food. Out of shyness, I would sit alone in a corner and eat my lunch. My initial years from 6th to 8th grade in high school passed in a similar manner. I, who once had no thoughts or worries about the reality around me, gradually began to constantly compare my situation with others, especially when I saw the parents of my classmates. Academically, I was an average student at that time. My interest shifted from mathematics to social studies and English, and I managed to score decent grades, thanks to my strong memory.

I pronounced English correctly and distinctly from the rest of my class. I enjoyed reading the Telugu newspaper at home, especially the science and technology updates section. As usual, I would talk to myself, imagine things, and dwell in my imaginary world. Teachers often chose me to give English speeches during the morning assembly. I always looked forward to participating in general knowledge and science quizzes. This significantly boosted my self confidence.

My father never took any real interest in my studies or what I was doing at school. Encouragement was out of the question—I never expected it, especially since he hadn't completed his own education. Instead, he had a way of turning everything into a joke or criticism, often laced with negativity.

I remember once going to a classmate's house to finish a homework assignment. When I came back, instead of asking how it went, he started mocking me in front of others, teasing that I must have gone there because I liked the girl. His tone was playful, but it stung. I had no such thoughts—it was purely about the homework. Still, the way he said it made me feel awkward and uncomfortable. I felt a strange mix of shame and shyness, as if I'd done something wrong when I hadn't.

That moment stayed with me—not just because of what he said, but because it made me realize how little he understood me. I wasn't just hurt; I was embarrassed. And that embarrassment slowly hardened into resentment. What I needed was support, someone to take me seriously. But instead, I became the punchline of a joke I didn't ask to be part of.

It's understandable if parents can't always boost their children's confidence, make them feel special, or motivate them. However, spreading negativity with narrow-minded thoughts, especially in the life of a child who is growing up without any support, is simply unacceptable.

I think this was the point in my life where I started questioning the existence of God and the unfairness of life. I even found myself asking why God had given me such parents. There was a time when I cried for hours behind closed doors, to the point where my tear glands nearly dried up. My aunt Chandrika was the only reason I could attend an English medium school and get basic essentials without any trouble. Even though she couldn't stay with me daily, she understood that my situation was different from other children due to my complicated parents. Once, in a fit of anger, I shouted at her, saying, "You are the reason my father has become so lazy." I don't know how she felt after hearing that or if she dismissed it as just a child's words, even though they were quite mature for my age.

Despite all the negativity, fear, and social anxiety, I managed to survive and push myself forward, fueled by the hope that I could achieve great things in life through my imagination. My aunt had a Nokia mobile phone back then, and it fascinated me because of my interest in new technology. She encouraged my curiosity, even when I caused trouble by blocking her phone with my experiments or making her pay a hefty postpaid bill by sending SMS messages to a TV program. She tolerated all my mischief with more patience than anyone else. I used to imagine running a mobile phone network, which became my favorite leisure time game when I was alone at home. I would create detailed plans, set tariff rates, and design promotional offers. This imaginative play allowed me to explore my interest in technology in a creative and engaging way. Looking back, it all seems so funny now.

By the time I reached 9th grade, my academics had improved further due to increased competitiveness and critical thinking. I participated in a district-level science fair, which required me to travel to a nearby town for the first time with my classmates and senior students. Despite my social anxiety and fear, I secured second place. Later, I even went on a school excursion to Bangalore and Tamil Nadu after convincing my aunt and others at home. I wanted to buy something special for my aunt Chandrika from Ooty, using the money she gave me for the trip, but I couldn't find the right item to purchase. I knew she was fond of sarees, elegant leather handbags, and watches, but at that moment, I couldn't come up with anything within my budget that would truly bring her joy.

During my high school years, she started visiting our house frequently after being transferred to a much closer location. During that time, I got to know her better. She was meticulous about many things—she would always place an extra bedsheet over the existing one before sleeping and often gave me advice on personal hygiene, studies, and other matters that no one else had ever shared with me. Reflecting on the past, it occurs to me that she may have had obsessive-compulsive disorder; this possibility sheds light on her decision to remain single and not share her life with a partner; it was at that time, however, that I began to perceive her as both a nurturing mother and a strong father figure.

She would always make time in her busy schedule for me like taking me to the dentist for my tooth decay and to the eye specialist. It was during these visits that I discovered my right eyeball is smaller than my left, although it's not noticeable from the outside. I can feel that my vision is primarily from my left eye. This condition is a result of my parents being cousins and marrying within the family.

My grandmother was diagnosed with a throat tumor, and since then, my aunt has been visiting our house more frequently. Sometimes, she even goes to work directly from our house, despite her office being in a nearby town. I entered 10th grade this year and resumed tuition after a five-year gap, thanks to a teacher named Yugandar who lives next door. With my aunt nearby, I was able to concentrate on my studies despite the usual chaos at home. I secured first place in the district-level science fair and achieved a respectable 90% in my 10th board exams.

My aunt knew me better than anyone else,including myself, understanding both my strengths and weaknesses. After my 10th board exam results, it was time for me to choose a stream for my intermediate studies (11th and 12th grade). Being a bookworm with little practical exposure and a lot of fear from growing up within the confines of four walls—never going out to play sports or ride a bike—I thought medicine would be a good fit for me. It requires rigorous studying, and at that time, I was confident in my ability to study for hours.

When I told her that I wanted to pursue BiPC (medicine), she immediately confronted me, saying, "You should take engineering. Your hands even shake when you hold a syringe; how can you handle knives in an operating theater? You're excellent with technology and computers—engineering is perfect for you." Reflecting on this, it amazes me how much my aunt observed me, noticing my nervousness and shaking hands—likely inherited from my mother, who also had this issue. No one else, not even my parents, ever paid attention to such details. From another perspective, it seems she knew that whatever career path I chose, she would be the one paying the college fees. Studying medicine (MBBS) is incredibly expensive, while engineering is a more affordable option. She might have considered this as well. Regardless, she had the insight to determine what would be the best fit for both of us.

As a result, I chose MPC instead of BiPC. The real challenge was leaving the confines of my home for the first time and moving to a different town, Rajahmundry, since there were no good colleges in our hometown offering technical education and coaching for engineering entrance exams. I was also named the best outgoing student by my school. With a mix of good, bad, and bittersweet memories, along with new hopes and fears, I prepared to move from my hometown.

The Labyrinth of Learning

My second aunt, Nirmala, who is a widow with two daughters, moved to Rajahmundry a couple of years before I completed my 10th grade to support her children's graduation. She has a very contentious relationship with everyone in the family. She had a property dispute with her own mother and she is always ready to criticize others.

Upon moving to Rajahmundry, I was initially supposed to stay in a hostel. This thought reignited the fear and social anxiety that I had developed over the years. As a result, I ended up staying at Nirmala's house, with my aunt Chandrika covering all my monthly expenses, including food, without telling me.

When I left home, my grandmother's tumor had progressed to throat cancer. My aunt Chandrika primarily worked from our hometown to care for my grandmother and my uncle, who had mental disabilities. She maintained a rented house near her workplace for her furniture and belongings, but seldom stayed there. My parents lived in the room that my grandfather once occupied, with its doors closed off from the rest of the house.

At my aunt Nirmala's house, I was provided with a small folding bed and a little space for my books. Feeling a blend of apprehension and excitement, I began attending college. I was placed in a special fast track class designed for students who excelled in their 10th board exams, as well as a few students whose parents paid extra to secure their spot in the fast-track batch.

In school, everyone knew me for years as the quiet, less social guy. Now, in college, I'm struggling to fit in among all the new faces. I've started sitting alone on the first bench, mostly keeping to myself. I should mention that my first year at college was quite structured, with me mostly confined to my books and bed at home. I maintained a regular sleep schedule, and since college is just a few steps away, I could easily go home for lunch.

I found myself surrounded by a diverse group of students, each with their own unique personality traits—some were very studious, others funny, some cunning, and some incredibly innocent. Many of them didn't even know I existed until the day I scored the top rank in the monthly test.

Since childhood, studies have been my anchor, helping me navigate through time without dwelling on my family, my past, or my future. Immersed in my books and facing increasing competition day by day, I became completely oblivious to what was happening back in my hometown, until the day my grandmother was admitted to a hospital in Rajahmundry. She had become so frail, almost reduced to a skeleton, unable to eat due to a throat tumor that had turned into cancer. She couldn't even speak properly. After a couple of days in the hospital, she passed away, and her body was taken back to our hometown.

This is the second death I've experienced involving people who have a direct impact on my life. When my grandfather passed away, I was too young to fully understand the situation. However, after my grandmother's demise, I realized that our extended family and distant relatives only gather during such tragic events, likely due to societal pressure to make an appearance. Otherwise, they rarely visit our home out of genuine family bonding.

Among everyone, I know that only my Aunt Chandrika truly felt the impact of losing her mother. She has spent all these years living with and supporting her parents, earning a living without getting married. I wonder if she ever thought about the possibility of being left alone after both of her parents passed away, especially given that her siblings lack a sense of kinship.

It is said that my grandmother's will states that our house will go to my uncle Srinivas, who is mentally challenged, and after him, it will pass to one of my cousins, my Aunt Sarala's daughter. This has made my other Aunt Nirmala and her daughters envious, leading them to discuss their share of the property with others, revealing their true intentions. I returned to Rajahmundry for college, staying at Aunt Nirmala's house, and life suddenly seemed to be changing. With Nirmala and her daughters constantly discussing money and property, I began to see a new side of family relations that I had never considered before. My Aunt Chandrika, now in the final years of her service, had no one to share her feelings and thoughts with while supporting my father and mentally challenged uncle.

Soon, my intermediate 1st-year final exams began, with the examination center located in Dowaleswaram, a few miles from Rajahmundry. There was a two-day gap between each exam. For the first exam, my father came to take me to the examination center from Rajahmundry, which upset my cousin, Nirmala's second daughter. The next day, she targeted me, calling my father uncivilized and saying I had no right to stay at their house. Although I didn't like staying there, I was just waiting for my exams to be completed. Due to this situation, I decided to pack my luggage, books, and everything else in the middle of my exams. My Aunt Chandrika arrived around midnight after her long day at work.

My aunt Chandrika was initially shocked when Harini, Nirmala's daughter, began shouting at both of us. She accused me of having no right to stay in their house and claimed that neither she nor my grandmother had ever given them any money or property, bringing up an old dispute between Nirmala and my grandmother over property. At first, Nirmala supported her daughter's outburst, but then attempted to calm her down—perhaps realizing that continuing the argument might jeopardize the monthly financial support my aunt Chandrika had been providing, or any future help she was hoping for. Eventually, around midnight, my aunt managed to find an auto-rickshaw, and the two of us left the house. Since my hometown was too far to reach at that hour, we headed to Kovvur, where my aunt used to work, and spent the night there.

I somehow managed to complete my Inter 1st Year exams, traveling back and forth between either Kovvur or my hometown. As that chapter ended, a crucial year lay ahead—for both me and my aunt Chandrika. I had to start looking for new accommodation for my 2nd Year, while my aunt was reflecting deeply on both my future and her own. With my grandmother no longer around, she felt she had no reason to stay in the hometown anymore, nor did she want to continue living alone in Kovvur.

Books and Bonds

During the summer break after my intermediate 1st year, my college continued to hold special classes for the fast-track batch. I attended these classes while staying with my Aunt Chandrika in Kovvur, commuting daily by bus. This period allowed me to observe her professional life more closely and learn more about her. She was meticulous about her office attire, blending decency and comfort in her sarees, and took great pride in being a working woman.

Despite her intellectual strength, she grappled with her own fears. Her parents, who had exploited her to support their unplanned and value-lacking family, were no longer alive. She was now responsible for a mentally challenged brother and an irresponsible brother who neither understood the value of money nor hard work, along with his troublesome wife. Her other siblings viewed her merely as a source of wealth, showing little concern for her true feelings. When I began living with her, she occasionally shared her frustrations and emotions with me. She once confided how embarrassed she felt due to my careless father's silly behavior at a family function she had taken him to. This is why she relied more on her subordinates than on my father or anyone else in the family.

Before my first-year summer break ended, she was transferred from Kovvur to Peddapuram. To ensure I could attend my second-year classes, she decided to rent a house in Rajahmundry and commute daily to Peddapuram. One of her subordinates assisted us in finding a house near my college, and thus, we began living together in Rajahmundry. The first 6-7 months in that house, with its spacious hall in the prime location of Rajahmundry, were among the happiest times of my life. I spent my days stress-free, focusing on my studies while sharing stories and thoughts with my aunt.

During this time, I made some wonderful friends and invited them to my home. Some even mistook Aunt Chandrika for my mother because she attended parent-teacher meetings. The beauty of college friendships lies in the fact that, despite the intense competition among us, we are actually competing against a much larger crowd at the national level to secure a good rank in the engineering entrance exam. There's no need for us to harbor immature jealousy towards one another. Those who don't understand this often struggle to make meaningful friendships, while those with realistic goals enjoy their college life, creating lasting memories and bonds, helping each other. You can achieve your life goals only when you focus on your own path, regardless of what's happening in the lives of those around you.

Sandeep and Manohar are two friends I bonded with effortlessly. We would laugh together for no reason, share the same bench, solve problems, and watch movies together. Nimshi, another friend who lived nearby, was a tech enthusiast. He introduced me to the Nokia Symbian OS, which was all the rage back then, as well as movies like The Matrix and books like Halliday Resnick Walker for Physics. As a boy with a vivid imagination, nurtured by spending time alone within four walls, I developed a deep interest in Chemistry. I often engaged in thought experiments, like Einstein, visualizing and creating my own theories about various chemistry topics and testing them while solving problems. Although I performed well in all three subjects—Math, Physics, and Chemistry—my Chemistry scores were consistently so high that I often topped the class, even if my Math and Physics scores were slightly lower. Whenever my aunt was at work, I spent most of my time at home with my books, thinking, or watching TV. Using the pocket money my aunt gave me, I bought many books from second-hand bookstores that Nimshi had shown me. This was also when I discovered the Harry Potter movies. Having already developed a keen interest in Hindu mythology from watching mythological movies with my grandparents during childhood, the Harry Potter movies added an extra layer of fantasy to my already imaginative mind.

While I was immersed in books and fantasy, the situation at home deteriorated. With my grandmother gone and my aunt now living away with me, there was no one to hold my parents accountable. The house, once livable, turned into a nightmare. My parents neglected cleaning and maintenance, opting to eat food from restaurants and watch TV. Meanwhile, my mentally challenged uncle wandered around, often not properly fed by my mother, who once secretly stole his sleeping pills but now does so openly.

One day, I found my aunt deeply upset. When I asked her what was wrong, she revealed that my father had sold the photocopy machine he bought with her money without informing her. I could see how angry and frustrated she was. It's important to respect and responsibly use the money earned through hard work, especially when you rely on others for financial support. Unfortunately, my father never learned this. Until then, I would at least say that my father ran a xerox shop whenever someone asked about his occupation. But after this incident, I felt so disheartened that I no longer knew what to say. Later, when my aunt mentioned that my father was asking for money to participate in local elections, I immediately advised her not to give him any. Despite me being just a teenager at the time, she valued my decision and denied his request.

As a child, I saw my aunt as an angel who visited during holidays to give gifts. However, after living with her for a few months, I came to understand her strengths, weaknesses, and vulnerabilities. Above all, I saw the human in her, with simple goals and dreams of living peacefully after retirement with whatever she had earned throughout her life. She even told me once that she plans to live with me after her retirement, wherever I may be. I wanted to tell her that once I got a job, I would take care of her well and that we could live happily, travel to many places, and do many more things together. However, I felt it was too early to make such promises without completing my studies and securing a good rank in the engineering entrance exams. While I was waiting for that moment and working hard to crack the exams, our lives took a different course, changing everything.

My aunt was diagnosed with a breast tumor and had to take medical leave to go to Hyderabad for treatment. She repeatedly assured me that it was a small, common tumor that could even be cured with home remedies like aloe vera and Noni fruit juice. She was influenced by Sarala and her husband, who were fond of homeopathic medicines. I really wished she would receive modern medical treatment as soon as possible, but I couldn't do anything at that moment. I remained alone in the rented house in Rajahmundry to complete my second-year exams

Crossroads of Fate

Having too much freedom and no supervision can be risky, especially when you have important goals to achieve. When my aunt Chandrika moved to Sarala's house in Hyderabad for treatment, my daily routine got disrupted, and I lost some focus on my studies. Despite this, my aunt made sure I had everything I needed by sending me pocket money. She also arranged for my other aunt, Nirmala, to provide me meals by sending her money separately, even though she faced humiliation at Nirmala's house. She did all this to ensure I didn't face any difficulties. I've also heard that my aunt Chandrika used to pay Nirmala's house rent during that time, but I'm not sure if that's true.

Until then, I had been studying almost stress-free without having to worry about anything. However, things started to feel stressful and disorganized when my daily routine was disrupted. I had a very important engineering entrance exam to prepare for, and knowing that my aunt was paying for everything despite being ill added to my stress. I often ate outside, consuming soft drinks and junk food whenever I felt hungry, as I didn't want to visit Nirmala's house frequently for food.

My house was cluttered with hundreds of cool drink bottles. Whenever I visited my hometown to stay with my parents, I was fed junk and outside food since my mother rarely cooked anything good. Even when she did cook, I wasn't accustomed to eating her food. Consequently, I continued living in the rented house in Rajahmundry, occasionally eating at Aunt Nirmala's house. I even fell ill frequently and often skipped college, which nearly led to my removal from the fast track batch towards the end of my second year.

Despite the challenges, I managed to do well in my second-year board exams. After the exams, my aunt Chandrika retired from her service, and her department arranged a retirement function. She traveled from Hyderabad to Rajahmundry to attend the event, accompanied by Sarala, who carried all her belongings, including her handbag, money, and cards. I also attended the retirement function. It was very disheartening to see someone who had struggled all her life to support her family, without enjoying much of her own money, attend her retirement function in such a weak condition. After the formalities were completed, she was taken back to Hyderabad to continue her treatment.

She even sold the land she bought at the beginning of her career in Tadepalligudem for a very low price to a group of people introduced by Geetha's husband to cover her treatment expenses. Initially, the land was meant to be sold to someone else, but after Geetha's husband's friends arrived, Aunt Chandrika was pressured by the family to change her mind and sell the land to them. As a result, the original buyers became furious and tried to intimidate her, causing her to lose several lakhs of rupees out of fear in such a vulnerable condition. Her other piece of land, which is adjacent to our house in our hometown, was registered as a gift to me before she left for Hyderabad.

That summer break after my second year was a crucial time for me, as the engineering entrance exam I had been anticipating was approaching. However, chaos surrounded me and my mind. I had to vacate the house I was living in because the owner was returning from abroad. Consequently, I had to move my aunt's furniture and belongings to a different flat. This new flat was in the same apartment complex where Nirmala and her daughters lived, and their criticism, filled with envy and greed, surrounded me once again. Amidst all the chaos, I took the entrance exam. In the examination hall, I suffered from a severe headache, likely because of dehydration and not having eaten enough breakfast. I couldn't concentrate properly and was really upset with my performance.

With all my exams completed, I no longer had a reason to stay in Rajahmundry and continue renting a house. Sarala, who now manages my aunt Chandrika's assets, vacated the house and shifted all of my aunt's belongings to Hyderabad. Since I was only waiting for my results and the start of my engineering counselling, I decided to visit Hyderabad and spend a few days with my aunt.

I was shocked to see that Sarala was living in a flat purchased by my aunt Chandrika, and even more surprising was the fact that she had made my aunt rent the adjacent flat just to store furniture and other belongings. This seemed completely unnecessary—the items could have easily been moved to my hometown, which is only a few miles from Rajahmundry, rather than transporting everything all the way to Hyderabad.

Still, I was there for my aunt Chandrika, and she was genuinely overjoyed to see me. Her love for me knows no bounds—even in her fragile condition, she took me shopping and bought me clothes. As much as I wanted to stay with her longer, I had to return to my hometown as my engineering counselling was about to begin.

As expected, I didn't secure a high enough rank in the engineering entrance exam to get into a government university. However, I did manage to get a decent rank—

good enough to gain admission to a reputable private college. The only thing left was to decide which stream of engineering to pursue.

My aunt had always hoped I would choose either Electronics and Communication or Computer Science. But during my intermediate studies, I had developed a genuine interest in pure sciences, particularly chemistry and physics. Unfortunately, pursuing a BSc in chemistry or physics wasn't seen as a viable option by most people around me. Engineering had become the go-to degree, regardless of what career path people eventually followed. Adding to that, the state government provided scholarships and fee reimbursement only for engineering students, as far as I knew at the time.

So, I decided to go with engineering. When it came to choosing a stream, I felt that Chemical Engineering would be the most suitable for me. It seemed like the only branch where I could integrate my knowledge of chemistry, physics, and mathematics. Without doing much research or considering long-term job prospects, I simply opted for all the Chemical Engineering courses offered by various colleges across the state.

During the counselling process, one of the officials at the counselling hall initially refused to consider me eligible for the fee reimbursement scheme, stating that my father didn't possess a white ration card—typically issued to low-income families. Hearing this, I was devastated. My aunt Chandrika was equally furious, especially knowing that my father had never bothered to apply for a white ration card, despite being unemployed for years and completely dependent on her support.

After a lot of pleading and presenting alternative documents to prove our financial status, I was eventually granted approval for the fee reimbursement.

Then came the results of the engineering counselling—I had secured admission in Chemical Engineering at Gayatri Vidya Parishad College in Visakhapatnam. Before leaving for college, I went to visit my aunt Chandrika. By then, she had been admitted to the hospital as an inpatient, undergoing chemotherapy. Her tumour had advanced into breast cancer. It was heartbreaking to see her like that. Had she started proper treatment earlier, instead of relying on homeopathy, things might not have reached this stage.

Even in such a fragile state, her concern wasn't for herself—it was for me. As I gently held her to support her while she tried to walk, she touched my forehead, worried that I might have a fever. That moment stayed with me—because maybe that's what real love looks like: worrying about someone else even when you're the one suffering.

Some distant relatives from Visakhapatnam were also visiting her at the same time. I overheard her softly ask them to look after me, saying I had no parental care. She never said these words to me directly, but in that moment, I truly felt it—that all these years, she had been trying to fill the emptiness left by parents who never really cared. And even now, at her lowest, her only thought was making sure I wouldn't be alone in this world.

With a heavy heart and holding onto the hope that she would recover, I prepared to leave for Visakhapatnam—the city where I was born, yet one I hadn't returned to since being brought back to my hometown as an infant.

The Edge of Comfort

On my first day of college, Aunt Nirmala accompanied me at Aunt Chandrika's request, since she had once lived in Visakhapatnam when her husband was alive. By the time I joined, classes had already begun and the college hostel was full, so I had to settle for a private hostel just outside the college gate. It was my first experience staying in a hostel, and I was anxious about how I'd get along with others, especially with my struggles with social anxiety. This time, I didn't have Aunt Chandrika to smooth things over like she often did in the past—but I also wanted her to believe I was doing fine on my own. The college was unusually strict compared to others, which thankfully helped me avoid the ordeal of ragging. At the hostel, I encountered a variety of personalities, but I mostly kept to myself.

In the classroom, I was able to do well academically. Thanks to my genuine interest in chemistry and physics, I naturally gravitated toward thought experiments—something I had always been good at. I performed well in subjects that involved theory and calculations. However, things changed when I had to step into the world of real-world experimentation—especially in the labs. I struggled with hands-on tasks, particularly in the engineering workshop, mainly because of my nervousness and trembling hands—something my aunt had always been concerned about.

One day, during a welding exercise, I had a close call. Despite wearing a protective shield, I accidentally exposed my eyes to the welding flames. For two terrifying days, I couldn't open my eyes and feared I had gone blind—but thankfully, I recovered. That experience shook me. I began to regret not taking my aunt's advice to choose computer science or something more suited to my strengths. I even skipped a few workshop sessions, just managing to maintain the minimum required marks and attendance in that lab. Still, I managed to score well in theory-based subjects and other lab courses.

At first, I was thrilled to watch movies with my hostel roommates and explore the city where I was born. However, over time, I began to feel fundamentally different from them. This feeling might have stemmed from comparing myself to them, especially when they spoke to their parents, particularly their mothers, while I only wanted to talk to my aunt. Additionally, I felt like I lacked any special talent. While others engaged in sports or pursued hobbies, I had nothing but a mind consumed by thoughts and overthinking.

My class is filled with people from all walks of life—from those born with a silver spoon to those whose parents endured years of struggle, hoping their child would one day land a stable job. I've always found it hard to place myself among them. My own parents were in a worse state than even the most financially challenged of my classmates. They relied entirely on my aunt's support, making no effort themselves. Yet, because of her, I never truly felt the weight of poverty. She made sure I had everything I needed for my education and basic needs. Still, deep down, I was always aware of how bleak things would have been without her in my life. Among my closest friends were Siva Krishna and Hari Krishna, who came from starkly different family backgrounds. Siva Krishna's father was a general manager at Hindustan Zinc, while Hari Krishna came from a modest rural family in Srikakulam.

While others spent their free time playing cricket or chatting about girls in class, I often found myself alone—wandering the streets or the hostel backyard, lost in my own thoughts. The few friends I had made during my intermediate years ended up in different colleges, pursuing branches like Civil or Electronics.

Maybe life is just a cycle of breaking out of the comfort zones we build for ourselves, if we truly want to move forward. I often felt like my family was broken, unlike any 'normal' family, and that left me with the sense that I was somehow different—destined to follow a different path. But I had no one to talk to, no one to open up to about what I was feeling.

Eventually, I built a new comfort zone: attending classes, returning to my hostel room, and keeping to myself. Over time, it seemed like everyone around me understood that I preferred silence—that I wasn't someone who spoke much.

Like in every stage of my schooling and earlier college life, academics were the constant thread that kept me going. It was the one thing that gave me direction, structure, and at times, even purpose. Through this focus, I connected with a few kindred spirits—like Siva Krishna, Hari Krishna and Bharath. Our bond was built not on small talk, but on shared curiosity: exchanging notes, diving into concepts, solving problems, and passing around books.

But because of my relatively reserved nature, I developed some differences with a few of my hostel mates towards the end of my first year of engineering, which led me to decide to move out of the hostel.

Initially, I moved into a rented room a few miles from my college with one of my hostel mates. However, shortly after we shifted, he decided to move out to stay with his classmates elsewhere, leaving me alone in the room. Fortunately, the house owners were kind enough to let me stay alone for another month, giving me time to find someone to share the room and split the rent.

Most of my classmates were either living in the college hostel or commuting from home, and since I didn't have a close friend circle, it was difficult to quickly find a roommate. During this period, my aunt Nirmala happened to visit Visakhapatnam for some personal work and asked if she could stay at my place for a couple of days, as she didn't want to stay with other distant relatives. Although I wasn't particularly fond of her, I agreed since I had stayed at her house in the past.

However, after she left, the house owner informed me that Nirmala had spoken negatively about my mother to them. I was furious—there was absolutely no reason for her to bring up or discuss my mother with the house owner, especially in such a way, that too in my absence. The owner didn't tell me exactly what Nirmala had said, but it seemed like she spoke very poorly about my mother. On one hand, I was furious with Nirmala for her cruel, sadistic, and ungrateful behavior. On the other hand, I couldn't stop wondering what Nirmala might have told the owner about my mother—perhaps that she steals things or doesn't keep the house clean. It made me feel so awful, as if no matter where I go or how hard I try, my parents and past always find a way to follow me and make my life miserable. I decided to cut ties with Nirmala and her daughters.

I began searching for a new place to stay and, fortunately, found a room with lower rent closer to my college within a few days. I moved in and started living alone. My new room owners were vegetarians and very conservative. The room, which had an attached toilet, was part of their house. They separated their living space from my room by closing a door. The only drawback was that I had to enter my room through the attached toilet, as I couldn't use the main entrance from their side of the house. As a result, I had to keep my toilet spotless to ensure that the entrance to my room remained clean.

Living under the supervision of a strict household helped me develop some much-needed organized habits, which were beneficial for my studies at the time. In my second year of B. Tech, I created a new comfort zone living alone in my room. I brought in Aunt Chandrika's custom-made bedding, a reclining chair, a large writing pad, and other items she had left in our hometown. Academically, I was doing well, consistently scoring decent percentages each semester. My analytical approach in chemistry, which had helped me during my intermediate studies, now aided me in excelling at chemical process calculations. As a result, my classmates and professors began to recognize me as a CPC expert.

During this period, I enjoyed the freedom of living alone and watched many movies, including Marvel's Avengers, often with classmates or sometimes even by myself. Occasionally, when Hari Krishna visited my room for group studies, we would go to the zoo or take a short trek to Kailashgiri on foot. Gazing at the statues of Parvati and Parameshwar on the hilltop, I often thought that perhaps the divine couple had taken the form of my aunt Chandrika to fill the void left by my parents. They treat everyone equally, and when they don't give something to someone, they balance it with something else.

During the first two years of engineering, I only managed to visit Aunt Chandrika in Hyderabad once. She had lost most of her hair due to chemotherapy and was very weak. I reassured her that I was doing fine, but I could still sense her concern for me. Even though she sent me money whenever I needed it, deep down, she probably always knew that my journey wouldn't be an easy one.

Where a Journey Begins, Another Ends

Two years and four semesters went by in a blur. I maintained a steady 80–82% each semester—respectable, but still behind the class toppers who consistently scored above 90%. Around that time, many of my classmates began preparing for the GRE, aiming to pursue their master's abroad. But for me, that path wasn't financially feasible unless I managed to secure a job through campus placements—not just to build a career, but also to start earning and ease the burden on my aunt.

However, deep down, I knew I wasn't suited for the chemical industry. At the same time, the idea of joining the IT sector didn't appeal to me either, especially since my chemical engineering degree would hold little value there. I hadn't made it to the IITs earlier, largely due to the turmoil I experienced during my second year of intermediate, and unlike many others, I didn't have the option of taking a gap year to prepare for the entrance exams. So, I set my sights on the GATE exam, hoping to get into a master's program at one of the IITs, and eventually carve out a future in research or teaching—fields where I felt my interests truly belonged, while also giving me a chance to earn through a more meaningful path.

I stayed focused on my goal, taking numerous mock tests and steadily improving my speed, all while maintaining decent marks in my semester exams. At that point, all I wished for was my aunt's speedy recovery and a good rank in GATE. But life rarely unfolds the way we hope.

Toward the end of my third year, my aunt's health began to decline. One day, I got a call from my father saying he was on his way to Hyderabad because her condition had become critical. I didn't know what to think or do—I just kept praying, hoping she would be okay. But within minutes, he called again. This time, his words shattered me: he was heading back to our hometown because my aunt had passed away.

It felt as if my world had come to an end. Memories of her flooded my mind; she gave me the love of a mother and the protection of a father, and I couldn't repay her in any way. Our shared dream of building a home and living together remained unfulfilled. I thought my tear glands had dried up after crying non-stop in childhood when I was bullied because of my mother. But now, with the news of my aunt's passing, tears rolled down my cheeks for the first time in over a decade and didn't stop all the way on the bus to my hometown, where my aunt's body was being brought. I arrived in my hometown at midnight, and my aunt's body was brought in the next morning. I never had the chance or the courage to tell her how much I loved her and what she meant to me. I cried and shouted that she was my true mother and father, hoping that at least her soul would hear me. In that moment, I felt an overwhelming sense of indebtedness to her, a debt I could never repay unless I could be reborn as her own child in her next life.

As the so-called relatives gathered for her funeral, their true intentions and opportunism became evident. It was revealed that while my aunt Chandrika was in Hyderabad for her treatment, she wanted to nominate me as her adopted heir. However, under the influence of Sarala's husband, who claimed she couldn't adopt me because I was a single child, she was persuaded to nominate Sarala's second daughter as her legal heir. Although I never desired any of my aunt's hard-earned money, I felt bad for her, knowing she couldn't enjoy it herself.

In an attempt to distance me from my aunt's property, Sarala even alleged that my mother had once spread rumors linking my aunt Chandrika with someone. Meanwhile, Nirmala and her daughters resurfaced their demands for a share of my aunt Chandrika's wealth. The entire scene was appalling, as they appeared no better than vultures fighting over a corpse.

Returning to Visakhapatnam with immense grief to continue my engineering studies, I felt blank and directionless, with my dreams of earning a job and taking care of my aunt shattered. Fortunately, I had already established a certain level of organized living that kept me going. To earn some money, I started offering science tuitions, as my aunt was no longer there to help me financially.

One day, I was contacted by personnel from the State Bank of Hyderabad. Upon arriving there, I learned that my aunt had a fixed deposit with my name as the nominee. They transferred the amount to my account. This was likely part of the money she had set aside for her treatment expenses after selling the land in Tadepalligudem. Perhaps this is what true love means. Even while battling cancer, she was thinking about me and my future, ensuring that I wouldn't face any problems even after her passing. Her care extended beyond her well-being, reflecting her deep love and concern for me. I opened a fixed deposit with that money, and the monthly interest helped me cover my rent and other expenses. This made me feel her presence around me, and I decided to focus on my GATE preparation.

Since childhood, I've faced complicated situations that I often struggled to express and convey to anyone. This includes my relationship with my mother, my father's irresponsibility, and now the loss of my aunt, who was like both a mother and father to me. Throughout my childhood, I often found myself lying about my mother and struggling to answer when people asked what my father did, knowing he did nothing. I've reached a point where I want to shout to the world that I can't lie about anything anymore.

Suddenly, I found myself unable to share my feelings with anyone. This helplessness even affected my campus interviews during my final year. I would try to express how much I missed my aunt during the HR round and ended up losing the interviews. However, since I didn't want to enter the IT sector or chemical industry, losing campus interviews didn't impact me much. I focused on my GATE preparation and was pleased with my performance, thanks to years of practice.

I scored an excellent rank in GATE, the best in my college, and was thrilled to finally pursue a master's program at an IIT and follow my dream of a career in research. With the same rank, I was shortlisted for PSU interviews with IOCL, GAIL, BPCL, and HPCL. However, I felt strongly that I didn't belong in the industry and couldn't work there, so I didn't take the interviews seriously. I skipped the GAIL interview, performed poorly in the BPCL and HPCL interviews, but the IOCL interview was not too challenging, mainly focusing on group discussions and a few technical questions.

I received admission offers for master's programs from all the top IITs and IISc Bangalore. I chose to join IISc, as it is considered the premier institute and center for scientific research.

As I prepared to join IISc with renewed hope, my distant grandfather called me to visit him in Vijayawada. I accepted his invitation and went to see him, which unexpectedly changed the course of my life.

Perception Rewritten

Narasimha Rao, the younger brother of my grandmother Savitri, lived in Vijayawada. He and his wife welcomed me warmly during my visit. He was genuinely pleased to hear that I had secured a good rank in GATE, and we had a thoughtful conversation about my future plans. I shared that I had attended a few PSU interviews and had also been admitted to IISc Bangalore. After hearing this, he spoke to his son—who was working in the revenue department—and advised me to consider joining a PSU, highlighting the attractive salary package, even though pursuing studies at IISc carried great prestige.

He then spoke with great admiration about my aunt Chandrika. He revealed that there had once been plans to marry her to another younger brother of my grandmother, but that man had died under mysterious circumstances—a story I had never heard before. As our conversation unfolded, he shared several such family stories that were entirely new to me. One of them was about my grandparents' marriage. He told me that, just as my grandfather was about to tie the knot, his mother suddenly intervened and asked him to step down from the mandap (the ceremonial wedding stage), claiming that the dowry had not been received on time. However, my grandfather refused to obey her and went ahead with the marriage. That moment, Narasimha Rao said, earned his deep respect for my grandfather. He then went on to draw a parallel between my father and my grandfather, saying that my father had inherited the same kindness and integrity—evident in how he stood by my mother, even when she became difficult to live with.

That conversation made me reconsider what my father must have been enduring while managing life with a difficult partner. I couldn't help but wonder how different things might have been for him—perhaps his financial situation would have been much better if my mother had been more responsible and emotionally stable. The meeting left me with a sense of renewal, as if I had begun to uncover parts of my family's past that had long been hidden. It felt like I was reconnecting with my roots. As I was preparing to leave, Narasimha Rao surprised me with a generous gift of ten thousand rupees—something I hadn't expected at all.

As expected, I wasn't selected for either BPCL or HPCL, and although the IOCL result was still pending, I had neither hope nor much interest in it by that point. Eventually, the day came for me to leave for IISc. Filled with excitement, I boarded the train and made my way to Bangalore, ready to begin a new chapter.

Stepping into the lush green campus and seeing the majestic buildings of IISc felt nothing short of a dream come true. Following the instructions I had received via email, I first reported to the campus hostel and got my room allotted. In the same hostel building, I met two other students who had joined the Electrical Engineering department a few days earlier. They were kind enough to help me buy a mattress and other basic necessities. After settling into my room and arranging my things, I casually checked my email—only to find a message from IOCL informing me that I had been selected. The mail stated that I was to report in Delhi within two weeks, after completing the required medical tests.

I was overwhelmed and unable to process this completely unexpected turn of events. My mind went blank. In a rush and just to be prepared, I had booked a Tatkal train ticket to my hometown for the next morning—train travel seemed the safest and most dependable option, especially since I wasn't familiar with the bus routes or other means of transport in Bangalore. I called my father and told him that I had been selected by IOCL, but I also shared that my heart was still set on continuing at IISc and pursuing a career in research, just as I had always envisioned. I wasn't sure how much he truly understood, but after a long pause, he simply said, "It's okay, do what you want—I'll manage. If needed, I can sell the piece of land that was gifted to me by your aunt Chandrika." His quiet acceptance and sacrifice struck me deeply. I convinced myself that things would work out, and that I could try to secure a job in research after completing my master's at IISc. With that, I made up my mind to stay and decided to submit my documents the next day.

The next day, I completed all the joining formalities and submitted my original GATE scorecard in the institute's main hall, along with many other incoming students. I was also scheduled for a medical test the following day, a routine requirement for staying on campus. That afternoon, I had lunch at one of the campus restaurants, where I met another student who had joined a different branch that very day. We decided to visit a nearby mall together in the evening. While we were there, I noticed him buying several items—including expensive perfumes and clothes—things I wouldn't have considered purchasing at that point in time. I assumed he must have strong financial support from his family. As we continued talking, I learned that he had previously worked at a company and had resigned to pursue his master's degree. Watching him, I couldn't help but wonder if I would ever achieve financial independence while still pursuing what I truly wanted in life.

That night, I received a call from Siva Krishna, who had joined the master's program at BITS Pilani. When he found out that I had chosen to stay at IISc and give up the IOCL offer, he said it was a foolish decision—noting that he was pursuing a master's degree only because he couldn't secure a job, and otherwise, he wouldn't have considered higher studies. His words left me conflicted. Even someone like Siva Krishna, whose father was financially well-settled, was anxious about money—while I had left my own father, who was already burdened with a difficult marriage and a mentally challenged brother to care for, considering selling a piece of land to support me.

For the first time, I truly began to grasp how crucial money is for survival. Until then, my aunt had always ensured I never felt the weight of our financial struggles—but now, it felt like poverty was creeping in, ready to consume me. Fear and uncertainty set in. I began to think that maybe I could work for a few years, support my parents, and return to pursue my master's later—just like the student I had met at the campus restaurant. Even though I didn't see myself as someone suited for the industry, I hoped that financial stability might bring some positive change in my parents' lives. With that thought, I made the difficult decision to leave IISc.

The Pigeon's Forgotten Window

It had been less than two days since I arrived at IISc, and I hadn't even attended a single class when I found myself needing to leave the campus. I was overwhelmed with worry, unsure of what to do or how to navigate my way out. I confided in the two hostelmates I had met on my first day, telling them I'd received a job offer from IOCL. At first, they were surprised that I was leaving so soon—but they sensed my helplessness and quickly offered to help.

They advised me to go to the main hall and request my GATE scorecard, which I would need to join IOCL. I followed their advice and approached the representative there. Initially, he dismissed my request, saying it had barely been two days since I'd joined, and that I couldn't be issued the scorecard yet. But after a long wait and repeated pleading, he eventually told me to get an application signed by the Head of my Department.

Without wasting time, I drafted an application stating that I needed the scorecard for an interview—intentionally avoiding mention of the job offer, fearing it might hurt my chances. I took it to the department, where the HOD, seemingly lost in his own work, signed it without paying much attention to what I said or had written.

When I returned to the main hall with the signed application, they took it from me and pointed to a massive stack of files piled up like a mountain. I was told to find my file myself, as the admissions had only just begun and the files hadn't been sorted yet. It was already lunchtime, and I hadn't even had breakfast that day—but I began searching, alone and exhausted. After a long and tiring search, I finally found my file and retrieved my GATE scorecard.

Back in my hostel room, I quietly packed my belongings, still unsure how I'd make my way home. The two hostelmates, who had become my anchors in a storm I hadn't expected, told me to catch an auto to the bus stand—where I might find a way to Vijayawada or Rajahmundry.

As they helped me with my bags, a pigeon fluttered into the room through an open window. But once inside, it panicked—unable to find the very path it had taken in. It flapped helplessly, circling walls and corners, forgetting the sky just behind it. One of the boys gently guided it back, pointing it toward the light. With a single beat of grace, it flew free.

So too did I.

I had entered that institute by choice—full of dreams, unaware that fear and duty would follow close behind. Now, I was leaving—not defeated, but redirected. Like the pigeon, I had needed a hand to find the way out.

As I stepped away from the place I once longed for, to stand beside my father in life's harder fight, challenges were waiting for me like winds against that pigeon's wings.

I boarded a bus to Rajahmundry, and from there continued on to my hometown, arriving the next day. My father was shocked to see me back so soon—but beneath the surprise, I could sense his quiet relief. He was happy that I had chosen to take up the job.

Still, I carried a storm of doubt within me, uncertain whether I had made the right choice. There was little time to dwell on it, though—I needed to complete a medical examination as required by IOCL. For that, I decided to seek help from Narasimha Rao's daughter and her husband, both doctors living in Kakinada.

I traveled to Kakinada with my father, where the doctor couple referred me to one of their clinics for a series of medical tests. The evaluations were extensive—especially challenging for someone like me, with poor eating habits, no involvement in sports, and a constant battle with self-doubt and low confidence. The results were concerning: my cholesterol levels were high, and I struggled with the Pulmonary Function Test (PFT), which assessed lung performance.

Fear gripped me. I worried that I might not clear the medical tests, and with my IISc admission already out of reach, I felt like I was running out of options. I requested Indian Oil Corporation (IOCL) for a delay in my joining date and was told I could report with the next batch, a month later.

That month was nothing short of torment. I drastically cut down my food intake, hoping to bring down my cholesterol levels, and rigorously practiced breathing exercises to improve my PFT results. Despite all my efforts, there came a moment when even my father mocked me for failing to do well in the PFT—without realizing that everything I was doing was, in fact, for him.

By the end of the extension period, I had somehow managed to get all my medical parameters within the acceptable range and boarded a train to Delhi. On the first day, I stayed at a schoolmate's place—he was working at an MNC in Noida. Knowing that I wasn't fluent in Hindi at the time, he helped me figure out how to reach Shahdara, where I was supposed to join IOCL. I joined IOCL at a five-star hotel in Shahdara.

Experiencing such grandeur for the first time filled me with a mix of emotions. While I was certain that many of my fellow joiners were also enjoying a luxurious stay for the first time, I felt anxious and sad as they relished the ambiance and food. My roommate at the hotel was from Kanpur, and I barely spoke to him during my stay,partly because of the language barrier and partly due to my reserved, antisocial nature. He shared his joy and experiences with his mom over the phone, while I missed my aunt. I wasn't in the habit of sharing anything with my father, as he never really cared about what was happening in my life. My only hope was that when I started earning, it would bring about a positive change in both my life and my parents' lives.

During the next fifteen days at the hotel, I was required to participate in numerous group activities. However, I mostly remained a silent spectator while others enjoyed themselves. The constant worry of having abandoned my dream career for money and status, which I couldn't share with anyone, weighed heavily on me. I missed my aunt deeply, so much so that one day, after returning to my room, I tried to hold back my tears by writing "Do not cry… Do not cry…" on a piece of paper, only to see tear drops staining the words.

As the 15-day induction program concluded, it was time for my posting to be revealed. I knew that wherever I was assigned, I would need to challenge myself every day to keep up with the world around me, overcoming years of trauma without my aunt, with whom I had always dreamt of living. Then, my posting letter was handed to me, revealing my posting in Bongaigaon, Assam.

A Whole New World

With fellow new joiners who were also posted to Bongaigaon, Assam, I boarded a flight for the first time. Along with the excitement, there was a new hope that I would be fine. In Assam, people welcomed us warmly, as we were the first batch of officers to be inducted at the Bongaigaon Oil Refinery. Our batch included individuals from IITs, NITs, and other prestigious institutions, which sometimes made me feel inadequate. However, I soon got busy adjusting to the new place. Most of my time was spent trying to learn Hindi by mimicking people, listening to Hindi songs, and searching for their meanings on the internet. The first few months flew by, and while some were transferred to other locations, a few of us were retained there.

I was assigned to operations-production, a role I initially thought I wouldn't be able to manage due to my tendency to get lost in thoughts and my reserved nature. However, over time, I began to cope. I realized that to grow in life, we need to break out of our comfort zones, and to live stress-free, we need to create new comfort zones wherever we are.

While my professional life was on autopilot, my personal life started to become complicated again. While most of my fellow officers focused on investments, I tried to give a significant portion of my salary to my father, hoping it would make my parents happy. When I visited home for the first time after being posted in Assam, I even pleaded with my mother not to take sleeping pills.

I wanted both my parents to maintain the house the way it used to be when my grandmother was alive—clean, organized, and filled with home-cooked meals instead of relying on food from hotels. Once I started earning, I was in a position to hire help, so I asked my father to arrange for a maid for cleaning and cooking, knowing my parents wouldn't manage these tasks themselves.

I also began doing what my aunt Chandrika used to do during my childhood—buying clothes and gifts for everyone at home. With my first salary, I gifted a few sarees to my mother and took my father to Rajahmundry to buy fabric for him and my uncle Srinivas, as he prefers to have his clothes stitched. I also gifted a saree to my aunt Geetha in Tanuku, who calls me more often than even my father to check on me.

At that time, I truly believed that my job and income would bring a positive change to our home. I hoped it would help me celebrate festivals with my father—just like every other normal family.

I was allotted a quarter in the township in Assam, and I was fortunate to have such warm and welcoming neighbours. One of the most beautiful things about Assamese people is their ability to find joy in the simplest moments of life. In my block, there were three other families—Hindu, Muslim, and Christian—and each of them showed me immense affection.

As a bachelor who didn't know how to cook, my downstairs neighbours, Hemen and his wife often invited me over for meals, especially. Despite the language barrier, I formed a close, family-like bond with them and their children. The warmth and kindness they extended to me made my time there truly special. I shared such a close bond with Hemen and his family that, on one occasion when I overslept early in the morning, I didn't hesitate to knock on their door. Without a second thought, Hemen's wife gently woke him up and asked him to drop me at the refinery—just like how a family would care for one of their own.

After my aunt passed away, my father took up a job at a courier office. Although his earnings were barely enough to cover his own expenses, I encouraged him to continue working for as long as he could. I believed it was better for him to be out and engaged in something, rather than spending the entire day at home with my mother and uncle.

During this time, Nirmala and her daughters filed a court case, seeking a share of my aunt Chandrika's PF and medical reimbursement money. These amounts had been given to Sarala, as her second daughter had been officially named as my aunt's adopted child—a decision that, I believe, was influenced during a time when my aunt was emotionally vulnerable and heavily dependent on those around her. The legal proceedings went on for several months, and my father and his siblings were repeatedly called to attend the hearings.

I urged my father not to get involved. To me, there was no peace in chasing after money when the person who mattered most—my aunt—was no longer with us. I was genuinely content with what she had left for me and my father. But it felt painful and deeply unjust to watch Nirmala and her daughters—who had once mistreated my aunt and even forced us out of their house in the middle of the night—now stepping forward to claim her money. The entire situation was disheartening.

Watching my father's siblings fight over money made me fear that, one day, they might even set their sights on the house he was living in. For now, as long as my uncle Srinivas—who is mentally unwell—is alive, no one dares to lay claim to the property, since no one is willing to take responsibility for his care. But I knew that if something were to happen to him, the same people might not hesitate to fight for the house—even over his lifeless body.

To prepare for such a possibility and ensure my father's security, I used my savings and the fixed deposit my aunt had left for me to purchase a flat in our hometown. My father rented it out and now receives a steady monthly income from it. Additionally, I created a fixed deposit in his name, so he could receive extra interest income each month to help cover his personal expenses.

He later proposed constructing a house on a piece of land he owned next to our existing home, taking advantage of a government housing scheme that offered partial financial assistance. I supported the plan by contributing an additional 4–5 lakh from my savings, in addition to the amount received through the scheme. The house was eventually completed and rented out as well.

Now that I was supporting him financially whenever he needed and he was also receiving additional income from rent and interest, he decided to quit his job at the courier office. I didn't object, hoping he would use that time to focus on more productive work at home.

But with money came its own set of problems. People like Nirmala and her daughters—who had once mistreated me—began seeking financial help through my aunt Geetha, who remained in regular contact with me. I would have certainly helped them within my capacity if they had approached me directly. However, when I asked Geetha to tell them to speak to me personally, Nirmala became furious and accused me of refusing to help despite having the means. She tried the same approach multiple times but never acknowledged her own behavior or mistakes.

Having witnessed the hatred and problems that money can bring from a very young age, I gradually lost interest in chasing wealth, exploring passive income streams, or investing in stocks and other ventures. I felt content with the salary I earned and didn't feel the need to pursue more.

Money Can't Tame Beasts

While Assam was treating me kindly, things back home in Andhra remained deeply unsettling. My mother continued relying on sleeping pills and refused to allow any maid to work at home. She had arguments with every maid my father tried to hire, often over trivial matters. As a result, both of them continued living in a neglected, almost unlivable house, increasingly dependent on outside food while letting the groceries they purchased go to waste. Meanwhile, my father began asking for more and more money without explaining how or where it was being spent.

Whenever I had to call my father and my mother answered the phone instead, I'd freeze for a moment. It felt so hard to even say her name. I'd just mumble, "Haa… it's me," avoiding any direct words, just hoping she'd understand and hand the phone over to my dad. That tiny moment always carried a weight I couldn't explain.

What hurt me the most was taking leave during festivals and going home, only to sit in an untidy house, eating junk food—just like the kind my mother used to give me when I was a child. The lack of comfort and care I longed for during those visits made going home feel more like a burden than a break.

I didn't have the courage or ability to open up about my complicated home situation to anyone at work or in the township. As time went on, my anxiety began to resurface. Combined with rotating shift duties, a disrupted sleep cycle, overthinking, and increasingly bad food habits, my health started to decline. Dark circles formed under my eyes, and I could feel both my body and mind beginning to wear down.

I grew so frustrated that I asked my father to vacate the rented flat and arranged some basic furniture there, so I'd have a place to stay whenever I visited my hometown. I also stopped sending him money blindly and instead began transferring a fixed amount while directly handling the utility bills myself. This upset him, and he began accusing me of taking away his financial freedom—something he had never truly earned or managed responsibly.

It felt like I had inherited the burden of fate from my aunt—forced to set aside all my dreams to support people who neither value my feelings nor recognize my hard work. My parents were incredibly fortunate to have my aunt sacrifice her life for their sake, and as if by cruel timing, the moment she passed, I stepped into a job that ended up funding their relentless, almost animalistic way of living.

Even if I wanted to keep my parents with me and help them understand what life truly means, I was burdened with an additional responsibility—my uncle. I couldn't bring him along with my parents to wherever I worked, nor could I leave him alone, as none of our so-called blood relatives were willing to care for him, not even for a few days.

I don't even have any siblings to share my pain or lighten the burden of my problems. I couldn't bring myself to abandon my parents and uncle to their fate as I was morally bound, no matter how much it cost me. It felt like I was trapped in a web of responsibilities with no way out, no practical solution in sight. What hurt even more was knowing that my father never cared enough to call just to ask how I was—unless he needed money.

Every day, countless thoughts would race through my mind. Sometimes, I would think about attempting GATE again and pursuing a master's degree. Other times, I would feel inspired by colleagues and start preparing for CAT or other MBA entrance exams. But none of it ever truly took off—there was no real driving force pushing me forward like there had been during my college days. Deep down, I knew that no matter how much I earned or how hard I worked, it would never be enough to bring real change in my parents or to create a space in this world that I could truly call home.

Some people, like Hemen Dada and his wife—who only knew a part of what I was going through—often thought I was overthinking everything. They would suggest that getting married might solve things. But deep down, I couldn't shake the feeling that no parent would willingly marry their daughter into a family with so many issues. Every parent wants a stable and healthy environment for their child. And I couldn't bring myself to share my burdens with someone else just to ease my own struggle—that felt too selfish.

Amidst the daily chaos in my mind, one day I received a call from my aunt Kalyani's husband. He surprised me by proposing that I marry their daughter, Vara Lakshmi. He even went on to mention that they had assets worth several crores, and since she was their only child, everything would eventually go to her. At first, I was shocked—he knew all too well about my mother and the situation in my family, yet he was still willing to offer his daughter's hand in marriage. But later, it began to make sense—they already knew me since childhood and were likely drawn by the fact that I had a stable job. There would be no need for explanations or justifications about my background. With all that in mind, I accepted the proposal.

Finding My Own Bridge

Varalakshmi was always a cheerful, carefree girl with a deep love for movies and film stars. She had a dusky complexion, while I was a bit fairer. Despite our differences, when I gently asked her whether she truly wanted to marry me or was being pressured into it, she smiled and assured me that she genuinely liked the idea. She seemed happy, and I believed her.

While I was getting ready to travel to my hometown to make further arrangements for the wedding, I unexpectedly received a message on Facebook from a girl named Yamini. She introduced herself as Varalakshmi's college friend from their engineering hostel. Yamini claimed that Varalakshmi was actually in love with a man named Rehman and had been hiding this from me. To prove her point, she even gave me the contact number of their hostel warden.

Confused and shaken, I decided to speak directly with the warden. However, the warden dismissed everything Yamini said and described her as someone with a bad reputation, intent on spoiling Varalakshmi's marriage. Still unsure of what to believe, I confronted Yamini. She seemed caught off guard by my response. I ended the conversation by blocking her and immediately told Varalakshmi about it. Varalakshmi was startled at first, but soon calmed down and firmly denied all of Yamini's accusations.

But just as I was trying to convince myself that everything was fine, a few days later, I received a call from my aunt Geetha. Her voice was trembling. She told me that Varalakshmi had eloped with someone, leaving aunt Kalyani and her husband devastated and heartbroken. A few days later, I learned that Varalakshmi had been brought back against her will, and her father had quickly arranged her marriage to one of her paternal cousins. The wedding took place quietly and within a very short time. After that, I never spoke to Aunt Kalyani or her husband again—I simply didn't know what to say. By the next year, Varalakshmi gave birth to a baby girl, and all I could do was feel happy for her from a distance.

That experience changed my outlook on marriage entirely. I believed that if I were upfront about my family situation, no parent would want their daughter to marry me—and if someone still agreed, I'd wonder what they were concealing. I also felt society had grown so tilted in favour of women that, should a future marriage fail—likely because of my parents—I could be left paying lifelong alimony.

But I knew I couldn't repeat the mistake my aunt Chandrika made. She chose not to marry, but she also never adopted anyone who could stand by her, support her, or encourage her to care for herself when she needed it most. In the end, all her hard-earned money went to people who saw her only as a source of income. I remained just her nephew—someone who saw both a mother and a father in her, yet was powerless to truly do anything for her. I don't want that to be my story. I want to have a child—someone I can pour all the love and care into that I longed for as a child. Someone to whom I can pass on not just whatever I earn, but also the life lessons and experiences I have gathered over the years.

I decided to discover what I truly needed in life before even thinking about having a child. So, I began traveling whenever I could take time off from work. My journey started with a visit to the Kamakhya Temple in Guwahati, and from there, I explored different parts of India whenever time and opportunity allowed. Since my parents rarely reached out—except when they needed money—I stopped going home. I spent the next few years traveling, observing people, taking photographs, and repeating the cycle. Even something as simple as watching people pass by in a busy airport brought me a quiet kind of joy.

With the advent of Instagram, I found myself drawn not just to photography, but also to words. I began pairing my images with quotes—thoughts that had long lived quietly in my mind, now finding form and expression. It was through this habit that I came to understand something deeper: pursuing an art form isn't merely a pastime. It's a vital means of expression—a way of reaching into oneself and speaking without words. Art comes in many forms, and each one gives us the power to convey emotions and experiences that ordinary conversation often fails to hold.

Everything felt just right—until one day, during a trip to Meghalaya, I took a trek to the living root bridge, and something changed.

One Step Forward, Two Steps Back

After my first promotion, I shifted to a new, larger, and newly renovated quarters. While the upgrade was nice, it also meant losing touch with my earlier neighbours. Though the new ones were kind, we were all caught up in our own busy lives. Work began to feel monotonous, and I longed for a break. I had always wanted to visit Meghalaya, so I spoke to my boss about taking leave, but he initially denied it. Fortunately, I later managed to get the leave approved and set off on a solo trip.

I reached Cherrapunji around midnight and, luckily, found a homestay despite the odd hour. The next morning, I began exploring the area's waterfalls. My cab driver took me to the starting point of the root bridge trek, where I hired a local guide to accompany me. The trek turned out to be far more exhausting than I had expected. At one point, the guide gently pointed out that I needed to improve my fitness if I wanted to continue enjoying such adventures.

He also shared stories from his village, where people still live without access to proper medical facilities. In emergencies—including childbirth—they have to carry patients up the hills on their shoulders to reach help. His words hit me hard. I had never paid attention to my health—no sports, no proper diet, and very little physical activity. For the first time, I realized that if I truly wanted to enjoy life, I needed to start taking my health and fitness seriously.

During the mandatory occupational health check-ups conducted every six months, my cholesterol levels were consistently borderline or high. The excess fat was even visible in the photos I clicked, often accompanied by acne. I even stopped posting any pictures of myself after a friend casually commented on my double chin. I always felt like I wasn't photogenic at all.

Changing habits I had grown up with was incredibly difficult, especially without any real motivation or inspiration. But in the end, neglecting my health—despite knowing that my eating habits would eventually lead to serious problems, felt like a slow, deliberate suicide tried making small changes, like going for walks and cutting down on sweets and junk food, but those efforts weren't enough to make a noticeable difference in my health.

Then I started noticing people like Rajat at work, who had gone through a significant transformation after joining the gym. His progress inspired me. But for someone like me—who had never participated in sports growing up, struggled with anxiety and overthinking, and lacked self-confidence—the idea of joining a gym was intimidating. The fear of being judged held me back.

Eventually, I found a solution. I chose to join a gym located a little farther from the township, one that no one from my office went to. It gave me the space to start at my own pace, away from familiar eyes and the fear of judgment.

The trainer was friendly and supportive. When he asked about my usual level of physical activity, I fibbed, claiming I walked a lot and even went for the occasional run. On my very first day he put me on a cardio circuit with a few others, and within half an hour I was so nauseous that I vomited right there in the gym. Thankfully, I could still make it back to my quarters on my own, but the whole episode was embarrassing.

Determined to turn my health around, I dragged myself back to the gym the very next day. The trainer and the other members hadn't expected me to return, but they welcomed me and suggested gentle cardio with longer rest breaks. That's how my fitness journey truly began. With their encouragement, I slowly built a consistent routine. For the first six or seven months I stuck exclusively to cardio, never even setting foot in the weight-lifting area. The process was both refreshing and transformative, and over time I could see—and feel—real changes in my body and my mindset.

While I was occupied with bringing structure and motivation into my own life, the situation at home continued to deteriorate. One day, all of a sudden,my father called to inform me that he had sold the house—the one built with government assistance and supplemented by my savings. I was stunned. Why would he sell a property when I had always sent him money whenever he needed it, and without even mentioning it to me beforehand?

At first, he offered a flimsy excuse: the house faced west, and according to vaastu, that orientation was inauspicious. I lost my temper and demanded to know why he had built there at all if the direction was so unfavorable—especially after spending my money and the government's grant. Cornered, he finally admitted the truth: he had been unable to collect rent from the tenant and, in a moment of helpless frustration, had sold the house for far less than it was worth.

The revelation infuriated me even more. Why dispose of a valuable asset at a loss instead of filing a police complaint against the tenant or at least informing me? The whole episode underscored how incapable and powerless he could be.

What angered me even more was that he gave Nirmala one lakh rupees merely to sign the sale papers, as the lawyer instructed, even though she had no legal claim to the land that my aunt had transferred exclusively to my father.

This reminded me of the time my aunt expressed her anger at my father for selling the photocopy machine that had been bought with her money—without even informing her. Back then, I only felt bad for her. But after this incident, I truly began to understand her pain—how it feels when your hard-earned money is misused by people who have no appreciation for the effort behind it.

When my granduncle, Narsimha Rao, once told me that my father was kind enough to tolerate my mother despite her difficult nature, I felt a sense of sympathy for him. But after this incident, I started seeing things differently. It was not kindness—it was incompetence and a lack of courage. If he had truly been strong, he would have walked away the moment he realised she was not the kind of woman who could support and nurture her children. Cowardice should never be mistaken for kindness.

Parenting My Parents

After this incident, I decided to limit the money I sent to my father, regardless of the situation. I asked him to clearly list his monthly needs, and I began transferring only the amount required for a three-member household. I also instructed him to place the money from the house sale into a fixed deposit and not to break it without my permission.

Over time, instead of acknowledging my hurt, he began to believe that I had become overly money-minded and was treating him this way simply because he was not earning. But from my perspective, I could no longer afford to act like a child to them. I had to become the parent—firm and responsible—dealing with children who had been reckless. Nothing else made sense anymore.

My parents spent a great deal on things they didn't need—unnecessary medicines, electricity from lights left on day and night, and food that ended up in the garbage. As I shifted to healthier eating, I hoped they would stop relying on outside food and start cooking simple, nutritious meals at home to save money and stay well. Whenever I went back home, I demonstrated things like how to sprout seeds and encouraged my father to follow the same diet I did. But they showed little interest in changing their habits; like children drawn to roadside junk food, they preferred their familiar, unhealthy routines.

I eventually reached a point where I realised that expecting them to change at this stage in life was not only futile, but also a drain on my time and energy—especially as I was nearing 30 and had my own life to focus on. Had I been working somewhere closer to my parents, things might have turned out very differently. But with most of my time spent far away and no siblings or anyone else around to look after them, there was only so much I could do from a distance.

Because mobile phones were prohibited inside the plant, I only checked for missed calls after returning to my quarters. My father rarely called unless he needed money, and I had no communication with my mother since childhood, so I often ignored his calls—unless there were multiple missed calls, which usually signaled something urgent.

One night, after reaching my room, I noticed several missed calls—not just from my father, but also from my aunt Geetha and a few unknown numbers. A sense of worry crept in. When I called back, I learned that my mother had fallen seriously ill. My father sounded completely helpless over the phone. I immediately informed my manager and booked the next available flight home.

Upon reaching my hometown and going to the hospital, I found my father sitting silently in a corner of the room, visibly anxious and lost. My mother was on IV drips. When I spoke to the doctor, he explained that her condition was too critical to be managed with the limited facilities available there and recommended immediate transfer to a multispecialty hospital in Rajahmundry.

I arranged for an ambulance and admitted her to the ICU in Rajahmundry, where doctors diagnosed a severe uterine infection. I arranged for an ambulance and admitted her to the ICU in Rajahmundry, where doctors diagnosed a severe uterine infection. She remained hospitalized for nearly ten days. I stayed in the hospital with her throughout, while my father occasionally returned to our hometown to take care of my uncle.

During this period,some of many relatives called to offer advice, mostly out of formality, but none stepped in to help—even with something as simple as checking on my uncle during such a difficult time.

No matter who my parents are or what they've done, they are the only people I have left in this world. Sometimes, I feel like a parent myself—trying to manage two spoiled children and one mentally challenged child, as if I have three kids to care for.

Throughout my childhood, I was kept apart from my parents. They lived in a separate rented house because my grandmother didn't approve of my mother. I hardly spoke to my mother, and I barely spent time with my father. I couldn't share anything with him, so I ended up seeing both of them through the lens of what others told me—mostly in a negative light. I never truly had the chance to know them, and they never had the chance to know me.

When I returned to Assam after my mother was discharged from the hospital, what worried me most was the thought that I might never get the opportunity to spend real time with my parents—to understand them, and to let them understand me.

Since chemical engineers are primarily posted in refineries, and Indian Oil Corporation does not operate any refineries in Andhra Pradesh, I had no opportunity to seek a transfer to my home state through the usual route. However, I was aware of exceptional cases, like a junior of mine who was transferred to the Visakhapatnam Marketing Division due to his wife's employment there. Drawing inspiration from such instances, I decided to write an application to the higher management, requesting a posting in the Marketing Division in Andhra Pradesh, citing my personal circumstances.

While I did not have the courage to explicitly mention my mother's history of drug abuse, I did refer to her mental health issues and the increasingly helpless condition of my father. I also highlighted the additional responsibility I bore in taking care of my uncle. Despite submitting the application, I never received a clear confirmation from the local HR regarding whether it was forwarded to the head office in Delhi. Filled with anxiety and desperation, I even travelled to Delhi to personally explain my situation to the management. Unfortunately, my efforts did not yield any results.

This situation dragged on for nearly two years, and over time, I almost gave up hope of securing a transfer on the grounds of my family's health issues. During this period, I found solace in working out at the gym, pursuing photography, and, most importantly, in the warmth and support of the people in Assam—especially the staff at my unit, who treated me like one of their own.

I never shared the full extent of my personal struggles with them and tried to maintain a cheerful demeanor as much as possible. But when they eventually learned that I was seeking a transfer to look after my parents, they sincerely wished the best for me and hoped I would be granted the opportunity I was striving for.

As I completed eight years of my tenure in Assam—without ever bringing my father there—and with the likelihood of a transfer growing stronger, even if not to a location of my choice, I felt it was time to take him to Assam for at least a few days. I believed that a short trip might bring a positive shift in both our lives.

However, the biggest concern was figuring out who would look after my mother and uncle in his absence. They had reached a point where their day-to-day survival seemed impossible without my father's constant support. I decided to test whether my mother could manage on her own for a short period, with minimal assistance from an outsider, just to see if such an arrangement was feasible.

Since it was December, I felt it was the perfect time to take my father with me to Assam, so we could celebrate the New Year together. I planned to bring him back around Pongal in January. To make sure things ran smoothly at home in my father's absence, I arranged my apartment watchman to deliver meals from a nearby hotel to my mother and uncle, and also pick up groceries as needed. I handed him the two-wheeler I had bought for my father and gave him separate funds for fuel. I also gave my mother some money in case of emergencies.

Interestingly, my mother readily agreed to stay alone once she had money in hand—it reminded me of how children behave. If you constantly restrict a child from handling money, thinking they're incapable, they may develop resentment or even a rebellious desire to steal. But when you trust them with money and the responsibility that comes with it, they feel empowered and happy. I believe my mother has been denied that sense of autonomy for years—perhaps due to how she was treated by my grandmother and by my maternal grandparents before marriage.

We had a landline at home for communication, and my father also collected a few of our neighbours' phone numbers in case my mother didn't respond to calls. Their help was important, especially to ensure my uncle was fed—since he tends to wander and, if not given food on time, sometimes visits neighbours' houses looking for something to eat. I also had my father prepare his clothes and essentials, and I booked flight tickets for the onward journey only, unsure how long he would be able to stay with me. I was still worried whether my mother could manage everything alone. And with that, everything was in place—I was finally ready to take my father to my workplace for the very first time.

Even Penguins Know

Knowing my father's inability to tolerate any kind of physical strain—even something as simple as sitting in one place for a few hours—I was mentally prepared for a challenging journey. Reaching my township takes nearly 15–20 hours, factoring in layovers and the travel time from the airport to my workplace. Still, I hadn't anticipated the unpleasant surprises that awaited me.

Early that morning, at Rajahmundry airport during the security check, I suddenly noticed a strong smell of alcohol coming from my father. Suspicious, I checked the Coke bottle he had brought with him and realized he had mixed alcohol in it. Shocked, I immediately asked him to discard the bottle. While I was disappointed and taken aback, I suspected he might have done it out of fear—afraid I would be angry if he had asked me directly. I kept my frustration in check, and we proceeded toward the boarding gates.

The rest of the day felt like travelling with a toddler—exhausting and unpredictable. After landing at Guwahati, I booked a cab to Bongaigaon, and by midnight we finally arrived at my township, where the cold was biting. I was slightly worried, knowing my father had never experienced temperatures below 10°C.

As we stepped out of the cab, to my horror, he nearly urinated by the roadside inside the township, unable to hold it for just another minute while I unlocked the door to my quarters. I was terrified at the thought of him creating an embarrassing scene in front of the neighbours—but thankfully, no one noticed. I rushed him inside, showed him the washroom, switched on the heater, and tried to make him feel as comfortable as possible.

The next few days unfolded just as I had expected. My father frequently complained about how I had arranged things in my house and criticized my eating habits—despite not having developed any consistent or healthy habits himself, apart from his deeply rooted superstitious beliefs. Almost every conversation between us would turn into a debate, but strangely, I found myself enjoying it. After all, I had rarely had the chance to just sit and talk with him in my entire life. We spoke about everything—from his life before marriage to moments from my childhood. I kept questioning him about many things that had always lingered in my mind: why he hadn't been able to manage my mother better, why he never seemed to plan for the future, and more.

He often brought up marriage, usually by comparing me to our neighbours who were already married. One day, frustrated, I asked him, "What if I get married and my wife isn't okay with me sending you money whenever you ask for it, like I've been doing all these years?" He paused for a moment and then casually replied, "Yeah, then you probably shouldn't marry. If you end up with a wife like that, how will I manage?"

That hit me hard. I was upset—more than I showed. For a while, I thought maybe he had started thinking about my future, because he later suggested I adopt a child. I almost believed he was genuinely concerned about me. I told him I'd consider marriage or adoption when I felt ready.

But then he said something that truly infuriated me—"If you don't marry or adopt, I'll adopt a child myself. That child will stay here with me, take care of me, and look after the property."

I was stunned. Here's a man who never earned enough to even support his own child, who lived most of his life relying on his sister and later on me—and now he wants to adopt a child just to use them like a caretaker? Just to make sure someone is around to serve him and protect property that he didn't even work for?

It was never really about me or my future. It was all about appearances—what the neighbours might say if his son didn't get married, and how to ensure someone was around to look after him and the property. Not once did he stop to think about what I wanted or how I felt.

Even when his careless words and irresponsible talk pushed me to the edge, I always held back my anger. Somewhere deep down, I kept hoping he would understand, that something might change. I even tried showing him wildlife documentaries—stories of penguins braving brutal winters to protect their young, salmon sacrificing their very lives to give birth, cheetahs patiently teaching their cubs to survive. I thought maybe, just maybe, he would see what true parenting looks like—even in the wild. That he would realize how even animals, with no language or wealth, give everything they have for their children. But nothing seemed to reach him. He watched those documentaries like a curious child, amused by the animals on the screen, but never once pausing to reflect. My effort to show him the deeper meaning behind those stories felt like throwing seeds on stone.

A few days later, I found out that my mother hadn't actually spent as much money as I had initially assumed. This only confirmed what I had suspected all along—that she had likely been taking money from the household not out of greed, but because she was never trusted with financial responsibility by anyone, not even my father or grandparents. I told my father bluntly that if he had earned decently and given her a role in managing the household finances with a sense of trust and accountability, she might never have felt the need to steal in the first place.

As I gradually improved my eating habits and tried to stick to a healthy diet, I encouraged my father to follow the same routine. Our meals mostly included brown rice, quinoa, boiled eggs, and plenty of fruits. Since neither of us really knew how to cook, we often ordered curries from nearby restaurants or occasionally ate at the township officers' club, which I felt was a relatively healthier option. While I went to work, my father usually spent his time roaming around the township or watching television. Though there were times when I felt low or upset because of something he had said, overall things seemed to be going fine—until one night during my shift, he called me on the office intercom and said he was unable to sleep. At first, I didn't think much of it. He had no fever or any troubling symptoms, so I simply told him to eat something—thinking a full stomach might help him settle down. But when I returned to my quarters, I found him restless and agitated. And then he asked me for the one thing I always hated to hear—a sleeping pill.

One Soul, Two lives

My father knew exactly how I felt about sleeping pills—he had seen me pleading with my mother to stop taking them ever since I got my first job. I had warned him so many times: don't take any medication without a doctor's advice, and stop giving her those pills.

So when I found out that he had secretly brought a few sleeping pills with him and had been taking them whenever I was at work—hiding it from me—I was shocked. He had gotten so used to them that he was now anxious and restless without one.

He never told me he had started taking them too. I was furious—but also felt helpless. Was it my fault for not expecting that he, too, would go down the same path as my mother? Or was it his fault for taking whatever he wanted without consulting a doctor or even talking openly about what he was going through?

I kept wondering—-what would I even say if I took him to the doctor? On one hand, I had years of bottled-up anger against this kind of medication abuse, and on the other, I couldn't bear to hear him say, "I can't live without sleeping pills." And I just stood there, torn between resentment and a strange kind of pity.

Later that afternoon, I went to a nearby pharmacy and asked if they could give me some sleeping pills. But the pharmacist refused, firmly stating that he couldn't dispense them without a prescription. Feeling helpless and unsure of what to do next, I headed back to my room on my scooty, my mind flooded with thoughts.

I began convincing myself to take my father to a doctor in the refinery township and ask for a proper prescription for sleeping pills. But just as I was approaching the junction in front of my quarters, everything changed in an instant—I met with an accident. I was left bleeding, with multiple abrasions, and my scooty was badly damaged.

The security guard who witnessed the accident rushed over and helped me get to the hospital, bringing my father along as well. My father looked visibly shaken by the incident, and for a moment, I thought he might finally be thinking beyond himself.

But as I lay on the hospital bed, receiving first aid for my wounds, he shifted his attention—not to me, but to his own discomfort. He began asking the doctor for sleeping pills.

I knew well that my father had little tolerance for even minor inconveniences and always sought comfort above all else. But in that moment, as I lay there bruised and bleeding, having narrowly escaped what could have been a fatal accident, it hurt deeply to see him more concerned about his own needs than the condition of his son.

It pierced something inside me—but I remained silent, because there was nothing I could do.

When I returned to my room, I tried to stay calm and reassured my father that I would somehow get him the sleeping tablets he wanted. I told him I would also make arrangements to send him back home with any colleague traveling to Andhra in the next few days. Desperate and mentally exhausted, I began texting all the doctor contacts I had, hoping someone would be able to help me get a prescription.

Meanwhile, my father didn't stop there—he even started asking our neighbours and colleagues who came by to check on me if they could help him get sleeping pills.

Trying to manage everything, I called a mechanic to repair my damaged scooty and asked him to take it to his shop. Just as I was sitting down, feeling overwhelmed and frustrated, one of my neighbours approached me. He told me, somewhat hesitantly, that my father had asked him if he could get him some alcohol. When the neighbour refused—saying he couldn't do anything behind my back—my father apparently left with the mechanic who had come to collect my scooty.

When the mechanic returned with my father, he quietly told me that my father had been asking him for alcohol—mostly through gestures, since he couldn't speak Assamese or Hindi. The mechanic said he had initially just shown him a wine shop, but once they got there, my father insisted, and because there were police nearby, the mechanic had to go in and buy the alcohol himself.

I felt a wave of shame and embarrassment crash over me. It hurt deeply—not because my father drank, but because he had gone around asking strangers and neighbours, people who barely knew us, instead of simply asking me. If he had just told me he wanted alcohol, I would have somehow arranged it, even if I didn't agree with it.

What hurt even more was the growing realization of the distance between us. Despite being father and son, there was such a painful communication gap. Had I become so stern, so intimidating, that he felt scared to open up to me? Did he really not trust me enough to share what he needed?

It broke something inside me—not just because of what he did, but because of how little he seemed to think before turning to everyone else around me, without once considering how that might make me feel.

Eventually, a doctor friend of mine managed to arrange a prescription, and one of my colleagues picked up the sleeping pills from the pharmacy. My father took them without a word and slipped into a deep sleep, as if nothing had happened.

I sat there beside him, bruised and bandaged—hurting not just physically, but far more on the inside. I stared at him, feeling hollow. In that moment, I couldn't help but think how pitiful my own situation had become.

Until then, I had always seen my parents as children—spoiled, directionless, unaware of what real life demanded. I believed they just needed guidance and discipline. But that evening, something in me shifted. I realised the truth was darker—they were both addicts. Alcohol and pills weren't just habits anymore; they had consumed them.

Even if some part of them still loved me, that love was buried so deep beneath their need for escape, it could no longer reach the surface. Their addiction had become their only emotion—their only priority. They no longer seemed capable of care, or concern, or connection. Just a need to numb themselves and disappear into sleep, leaving the rest of the world—including me—on mute.

When my father finally woke up later that day, I couldn't hold it in anymore. I asked him quietly, "What if one day I die here, and you have to come all the way from Andhra just to collect my body?"

He looked at me and said, "I'll bring sleeping pills with me too."

I didn't know whether he meant it seriously or if he even understood what he was saying. But hearing those words broke something inside me. In that moment, I didn't feel like a son—I felt invisible. Unloved. Unwanted. As if my life, or even my death, wouldn't mean anything beyond being another inconvenience in his troubled world.

I couldn't bear seeing my father in front of me any longer. I tried to send him home alone by train, but I couldn't even manage a tatkal ticket. And I knew—deep down—that someone like him, worn down by addiction and dependency, couldn't possibly endure a 35–40 hour train journey on his own.

So, despite my unhealed wounds and exhausted body, I booked flight tickets for both of us. I decided I would at least take him as far as Hyderabad and put him on a bus from there. I stayed calm throughout the journey, holding back everything I was feeling. When we reached, I handed him some money, ensured he boarded the bus safely, and watched as it pulled away into the night.

And then I was left standing there—alone on a dimly lit highway, broken in ways I couldn't put into words. That's when it truly sank in: my aunt and I were never loved, not really. We were just cash dispensers to our family—machines expected to function, to give, to sacrifice, while never being allowed to dream, to feel, or to ask for anything in return.

Her cursed legacy didn't end with her. It lives on in me. We were never two different souls. We were always one—one tired soul trapped in two different bodies. This isn't a tale of two lives. It's the story of a single soul, echoing through both of us, quietly enduring, endlessly giving… and still, unheard, unloved…..

www.ingramcontent.com/pod-product-compliance
Lightning Source LLC
Chambersburg PA
CBHW050020170726
48282CB00025B/477
* 9 7 8 9 3 3 4 3 5 0 1 0 4 *